CONSPIRACIES & BRAINWASHING

THE EPISTLE OF NAPOLEON
TO THE DINOSAURS

DEADMAN SWITCH

Outskirts Press, Inc.
Denver, Colorado

Conspiracies & Brainwashing
The Epistle of Napoleon to the Dinosaurs
All Rights Reserved.
Copyright © 2008 Deadman Switch
V1.0

Outskirts Press, Inc.
http://www.outskirtspress.com

ISBN: 978-1-4327-2906-6

Library of Congress Control Number: 2008933713

Outskirts Press and the "OP" logo are trademarks belonging to Outskirts Press, Inc.

PRINTED IN THE UNITED STATES OF AMERICA

TABLE OF CONTENTS

Chapter 1   Basic Truths of Conspiracies 1

Chapter 2   The Rules of The Game 3

Chapter 3   Brainwashing 7

Chapter 4   Conspirators and Non-Conspirators...19

Chapter 5   Differences Between Conspiracies 25

Chapter 6   Alas, Babylon....................................35

Chapter 7   Proof 39

Chapter 8   Stuff the Feds Mess With..................52

Chapter 9   Code 81

Chapter 10   What Really Happened 104
             Sept. 11th, 2001

Restatement Postscript 109

CHAPTER 1
BASIC TRUTHS OF CONSPIRACIES

1. People are social creatures who form groups.
2. Any group becomes a conspiracy when they keep a secret.
3. A conspiracy is still a conspiracy even if:
    B. It is called by another name. Examples: revolutionary movements, urban gangs, political cover-ups, terrorist networks, "old boy" networks, organized crime.
    C. It isn't doing anything unlawful or harmful. Example: a surprise party.
    D. It is impossible to expose it. Example: American traitors helping Russia win a nuclear war.
    E. It is exposed and goes public. Example: the Ku Klux Klan.
4. Everyone knows that conspiracies exist but no one believes in them.
5. Honest people don't believe in conspiracies because every honest person is brainwashed.
6. How to brainwash people is a conspiracy secret.
7. Small and medium sized conspiracies are usu-

ally sub-groups of much larger conspiracies.

8. Larger conspiracies are more dangerous and less likely to be exposed than small conspiracies. Larger conspiracies have greater offensive and defensive capabilities.

9. A. Published information about conspiracies is invariably incomplete and misleading.

   B. All public communications media are controlled by conspiracies.

   C. Publicity to expose a conspiracy always comes from a conspiracy.

10. The only way to fight a conspiracy is with another conspiracy.

11. Every type of death and destruction comes from conspiracies fighting for power.

12. For those who fight for power, the ultimate objective is to rule the world.

CHAPTER 2
THE RULES OF THE GAME

The Federation conspiracy has rules about keeping secrets. The main points are:

1. Anyone who is invited to join a conspiracy and refuses must be killed.
2. Anyone else who isn't a conspirator who finds out the truth about conspiracies must be killed.
3. Anyone who isn't a conspirator who finds out the truth about brainwashing must be killed.
4. Anyone who isn't a conspirator who finds out that they are brainwashed; enslaved by mind control, must be killed.
5. Anyone who attempts to expose conspiracies by offering proof of their existence must be killed.

This includes innocent people who accidentally discover proof of conspiracy secrets, but it doesn't include anyone with theories but no proof. You can also keep quiet about what you know and escape death sometimes, provided that the Feds don't find out and whoever has you brainwashed doesn't want you killed. Whoever has you brainwashed can read your mind; you cannot keep any secrets from them.

For the past fifteen hundred years the Feds have dealt with anyone who breaks the rules by keeping them under surveillance and gathering information about them for 30 days and then killing them in a manner which doesn't seem to be murder. During the second half of the twentieth century they normally used poisons which produce heart attacks and strokes. The heart attack poison is a derivative of nerve gas, in the form of a drop of liquid which is absorbed through the skin.

The conspiracies have rules about warning each other of an impending operation or attack. The warnings are broadcast by books, movies, TV shows, and songs which describe a situation that might arise or something that a conspiracy might have to do. The warnings don't describe what the enemy will do to produce that situation, just the results. For example: The Manchurian Candidate was a warning to the Feds from the Mafia of the situation that would result from the assassination of President Kennedy. The actors are usually, but not necessarily always, members of the conspiracy that is being warned. The author and director might be either from the conspiracy that is being warned or from the conspiracy that is giving the warning.

There seems to be a rule about how to assassinate a political leader. The assailant must use a handgun, while in full view in a public place, and must be portrayed as insane or a member of the lunatic fringe. But several different assassinations broke that rule.

The Feds assassinated Franklin Delano Roosevelt because he planned to keep the atomic bomb a secret and defeat Japan without using it. The Feds were planning for the Russians to win a nuclear war against the United States, and wanted the atomic bomb used and publicized so that Russia could develop atomic bombs. They probably used poison because of a combination of circumstances. They had a newly developed poison available, they wanted to demonstrate it to their enemies, using it would keep somebody from being held responsible for a breach of security during wartime, and using it would keep everyone except conspirators from wondering why Roosevelt was murdered. The Mafia broke the rule for the assassination of President Kennedy because they needed to frame Lee Harvey Oswald. I don't know why the rule was broken for the assassination of Anwar El Sadat.

While George Bush (Sr.) was President, there was a series of lethal accidents on U.S. Navy ships. Then President Bush was invited to a summit meeting with Gorbachev aboard naval warships in the Mediterranean. At the news conference to announce the summit meeting, President Bush gave a hand signal, wiping a tear from beneath your eye, which translates as "They're going to kill me." At the summit meeting, a storm produced high waves. It had been planned to take President Bush from his ship to Gorbachev's ship with a small boat. The waves broke the boarding ladder used to board the small boat. When President Bush explained to Gorbachev that the broken boarding ladder kept him from visiting the Russian ship, Gorbachev snapped "You should teach your sailors to repair." The accidents on U.S. ships during the preceding months had established plausible deniability for an accident on a Russian ship which was intended to kill President Bush. They might not have wanted to shoot him in the usual manner because it would have meant more gun control laws. The motive might have been retaliation.

The Mafia has a rule that you have to earn your position. I suppose that means you have to prove that you can do that job.

There are probably lots of other rules that I don't know.

CHAPTER 3
BRAINWASHING

Brainwashing has been called by many different names. Two thousand years ago it was called being possessed by a demon or a devil. One thousand years ago it was called witchcraft, or being put under a spell. No matter what it is called, it is always the same type of mind control, and it is older than recorded history. The correct term these days is hypnosis. Brainwashing is just a euphemism for hypnosis.

The human brain is capable of different levels of consciousness. A child less than four or five years old has a brain wave pattern different from that of an adult. Some types of stimuli can cause the adult brain to revert to that original level of consciousness. It is possible to hypnotize someone without their knowledge and consent because the conscious mind normally doesn't remember what happens while the brain is operating at the other level. In order to hypnotize someone, you must apply a stimulus to cause their brain to revert (or just be present when it happens to them), and then implant a signal so that their brain will revert just from the signal.

The signal can be something that the victim sees, or hears, or smells, or tastes, or feels, or any combination.

There are three types of hypnosis because there are three basic types of stimuli that can cause the brain to revert. The separate discovery of each type of hypnosis during prehistory produced three separate conspiracies. The Biblical names for the three conspiracies are: the kingdom, the power, and the glory, or: the kings, the beast, and the whore. The common names are: the Feds, the Nazis, and the Mafia. For other names see Chapter 9 Code.

The first method of hypnosis is trauma. Anything painful enough or frightening enough or traumatic enough sends you into shock. That is Nazi hypnosis. Wounded men in great pain go into shock and call out for their mother because their brain has reverted to childhood. They don't remember it afterward; to them it seemed that they became unconscious. Nazis use torture, beatings, threats, phobias, and verbal assaults.

"The Voice" from the book Dune by Frank Herbert is verbal assault; suddenly using an urgently threatening voice to scare someone. It works best on children, but law enforcement officers use it on adults too. It is made more effective by having something to threaten the intended victim with, and the power to make the threat come true.

The incident with the rats from the book Nineteen Eighty-four by George Orwell is phobia hypnosis. You shouldn't ever tell anyone what you are afraid of because it could be used to hypnotize you. The scene from The Parallax View where Warren

Beatty is shown a series of pictures demonstrates a method of finding out what you are afraid of. If you see something you like, the pupils of your eyes dilate. If you see something you don't like, your pupils contract. They watch your eyes to find out what you are afraid of. That phenomenon is very useful for conspirators. It can help them hypnotize you, it can tell them whether you are under hypnosis at the moment, and it can tell them which method of hypnosis is being used on you.

The most widely effective methods of Nazi hypnosis are torture, beatings, and canings. The Egyptian that Moses murdered was beating Hebrews to hypnotize them. In Nazi controlled countries the government authorities torture prisoners because that is how they hypnotize and enslave people. All depending on the circumstances, a prisoner who has been hypnotized by torture may forget that he was tortured. People who are hypnotized by Nazis under other circumstances normally don't remember what was done to them to hypnotize them. People who are hypnotized by Mafia and Feds remember what happened, but aren't aware that it hypnotized them.

The second method of hypnosis is pleasure. Anything pleasurable enough sends you into shock, and if there is a conspirator around, you get hypnotized. That is Mafia hypnosis. Examples: losing your virginity, oral sex the first or second time, having a whore satisfy your sexual fetish, exciting forbidden sex, anything that turns you on so much that you have an orgasm immediately. Actually you went under hypnosis, and had the orgasm when you came back to normal consciousness.

Everyone develops a sexual fetish during childhood from instinct. Most four-footed animals mate by scent, but birds and people fixate on visual signals. Girls get a sexual fetish for something they see their father doing when they are five or six years old, boys get a sexual fetish for something they see their mother doing when they are seven or eight years old. But sometimes a child gets a sexual fetish for something done by someone other than the parent of the opposite sex, usually because of an abnormal home environment. Pornography catering to someone's sexual fetish is what the Bible calls idolatry. Whores use it to hypnotize people.

The Mafia also uses drugs and alcohol, good-tasting food and drink, music, jokes and humor, and recreational activities. Anything pleasurable is addictive. It isn't a coincidence that the Surgeon General is against everything you enjoy. The Feds want to destroy everything that the Mafia uses.

Fed hypnosis is the method that everyone has heard of. Relax; concentrate, while listening to the voice of the master. Moses learned this method and used it to free the Hebrews from slavery. Examples: eye tests, hearing tests, confessional booth, someone teaching you to read, someone teaching you to sew, someone teaching you to tie flies, teaching you to play a game, or giving you a massage. An ancient technique from the Orient is a spinning disk with a spiral painted on it; computer games are the most modern method.

The hypnotist talks in an authoritative, calm, soothing monotone with a deliberate-tempo-and-interval-between-words. It is said that the hypnotist should have prestige; that is, a status which commands respect and obedience. If the hypnotist doesn't have prestige or the right kind of voice, devices which help focus the subject's attention are likely to be used. The first time I was hypnotized with Fed hypnosis I agreed to be hypnotized so a tape-recorded relaxation routine was used. The hypnotist did not admit that the attempt was successful and I did not have any memory of having been under hypnosis.

The Feds also have a device which causes the brain to revert by blinking light at brain wave frequencies. I have seen depictions of devices which flash light to hypnotize people three different times. See the movie Looker starring Albert Finney and Susan Dey, the Star Trek; The Next Generation episode The Game, and the movie Men In Black.

During the late 1960's or early 1970's I read a book which had a brief mention of how it was discovered. Many single-engine planes crashed while landing at an airport runway that was lined up with the setting sun. The Fed investigators discovered that when the plane's propeller was turning at the right speed, the blinking put the pilot under hypnosis, which caused the plane to crash.

The light has to be very bright. The rate at which it blinks probably has to decrease from the upper limit of the cycles per second of Beta brain waves down to the lower limit of the cycles per second of Alpha brain waves. According to the information I've been able to find, that is from 30 cycles per second down to 8 cycles per second. But if you really want to know how it works, the proper starting point for research would be to obtain a number of electroencephalograms of children under the age of four, adults in normal consciousness, and adults under hypnosis.

Most people are immune to some kinds of hypnosis because some methods work just once, but no one is immune to that blinking light because it acts directly on the brain. It will hypnotize anyone except very young children whose brains aren't operating on Beta waves.

Hypnosis is a condition of induced monomania. The stimulus that is being used becomes the most important thing to the subconscious mind, and the subconscious mind controls the conscious mind.

Conspirators often lie to their hypnotized subjects and create a false scenario to get them to do something which they would ordinarily refuse to do. While you are under hypnosis you are living in a dream world that was created by your hypnotist. You sometimes dream something you did while hypnotized that your conscious mind doesn't remember. To get you to do something unlawful, they create a dream in which it is lawful.

Usually when they hypnotize someone into committing a crime, they arrange for him to remember it afterward. The perpetrator commits the crime while under hypnosis and then comes out of hypnosis. He continues his normal life without remembering he did it. Then the policeman says "Freeze!" and he remembers it. Once he remembers it, it feels just as if he remembered it all along. But occasionally the police cannot hypnotize him into remembering it. Then he says he was framed. Nope. He did it; he just doesn't remember it because it happened while he was under hypnosis.

Hypnosis is dishonest and evil. The reason for hypnotizing someone is to get them to do what you want. The hypnotist is responsible for what the hypnotized person does. Jesus forgave the sins of hypnotized people. The hypocrites He condemned were conspirators.

Hypnosis is responsible for every mental aberration. Any incident in which someone did something without remembering it was from hypnosis. Multiple personalities, repressed memories, amnesia, and sleepwalking are caused by hypnosis. Those are mental problems which psychologists treat with hypnosis because they were caused by hypnosis.

People who are under hypnosis look normal, and can talk normally, but act just slightly different from normal. Each time they hypnotize you with a different method they can create a different personality. For example: In the book The Three Faces of Eve, the personality called Eve White is from Nazi hypnosis, Eve Black is from Mafia hypnosis, and Jane is from Fed hypnosis. But it isn't just different conspiracies. Nazis could hypnotize a young child with verbal assault to create the first alternate personality, hypnotize him with phobia hypnosis to create the second personality, have him caned at school to create the third personality, and hypnotize him with sex hypnosis after he reaches puberty to create the fourth personality.

Repressed memories are usually discovered when someone who had previously been hypnotized by Mafia or Nazis gets hypnotized by the Feds. The Fed hypnotist uses hypnosis to review the entire life of the hypnotized person. He wants to know their likes and dislikes, their talents and ambitions, what they were trained to do or used for by the other conspiracy, and to find and delete the hypnosis signals implanted by the other conspiracy. He learns that the hypnotized person while under hypnosis witnessed a crime committed by the Mafia or Nazis. He wants his enemies to be punished for the crime, but he cannot admit that he learned of it by hypnotizing someone. So he hypnotizes his subject into remembering and reporting the crime.

Picture a string of dominoes laid out lengthwise. Each domino represents a memory of an event of your life. Some of the dominoes are face up, with the dots showing. Those are memories of events while you were conscious. Some of the dominoes are face down, with the dots hidden. Those are memories of events while you were under hypnosis. To you it seems that you have an unbroken string of face up dominoes. Actually, there are face down dominoes inserted here and there. Your hypnotist flips one of them face up, and you remember something that happened while you were under hypnosis. You might be able to recognize a hypnosis memory if you can recall the feeling of monomania which was controlling you. Otherwise you are not likely to be able to tell the difference unless your hypnotist wants you to.

I don't know how hypnosis causes amnesia, but I can think of a couple of possibilities. The hypnotist could order the hypnotized person to forget, or could cause their time sense to regress and leave it regressed. Hypnosis has been used for criminal investigation by causing someone to re-live an incident in order to obtain information about it. Reasons for giving someone amnesia might include getting them to do something they wouldn't have done if they hadn't had amnesia, keeping them from doing something they would have done if they hadn't had amnesia, or hiding criminal activity.

Whenever someone performs purposeful acts while asleep they were actually under hypnosis, but I just don't know enough about it to explain how and why.

Hypnosis can be used to perform magic tricks. Any hypnotist can make any movable object appear or disappear right before the eyes of his hypnotized subject by putting the subject under hypnosis, producing or removing the object, and bringing the subject back to normal consciousness.

Once I was in a room with two windows in the wall toward the public street. I saw an automobile traveling up the road in one of the windows. When it went behind the section of wall between the windows, I looked at the second window and watched for it to appear. It failed to appear. I went to the window and looked up and down the road and it had disappeared. The explanation is that I went under hypnosis during the few seconds that the automobile was between windows, and stayed under hypnosis long enough for it to travel up the road out of sight. Then I came back to normal consciousness and resumed what I had been doing without being aware of any interruption. There wasn't any feeling of having been under hypnosis, just the disappearance to prove it.

Afterward the conspirator who owned that house kept the windows covered with Venetian blinds. That proves it was from hypnosis. I did not mention the incident to anyone for several months, so how did he know about it? He learned of it by hypnotizing me. No matter how he learned of it, he would not have covered the windows because of someone else's spontaneous mental aberration. He covered the windows to avoid having to watch for automobiles each time he intended to hypnotize me.

Hypnosis causes people to see things that aren't there, such as flying saucers, and causes them to be blind to what is there. You cannot see an object or understand an idea if your hypnotist doesn't want you to. That's why conspirators use the word "blind" to refer to hypnotized people.

Your hypnotist can be in your blind spot too. I now know that I was hypnotized by Nazis who weren't members of my family while I was between the ages of eight and eighteen. They had to meet with me to hypnotize me, but I didn't ever see any of them. If you suspect that your child is hypnotized by someone who isn't a member of your family, watch to see who meets with them, and ask them if they remember it.

Hypnosis causes the symptoms of brainwashed people; sudden changes of beliefs and priorities, irrational opinions, an inability to understand what you try to explain to them, anger if you keep trying to explain it, and doing things that aren't in their own best interest.

If you argue with their irrationality they become angry because you are threatening something that is very important to their subconscious mind. They do things that aren't in their own best interest because they are doing things that are in the best interest of their hypnotist, or in the best interest of the conspiracy that their hypnotist belongs to.

All three methods of hypnosis have one thing in common; they get all of your attention. Something very painful or very frightening gets all of your attention, and so does something intensely pleasurable. Being forewarned isn't a defense against those methods, but it is against Fed hypnosis. A good subject for Fed hypnosis is a trusting person with the ability to concentrate. If you are careful not to concentrate and don't trust anyone it will be difficult for the Feds to hypnotize you with their usual methods.

The best defense against hypnosis is to escape from your hypnotists. If they cannot find you they cannot give you signals to put you under hypnosis. You must run away immediately after deciding to, without having any contact with anyone you are acquainted with. If you delay running away your hypnotist will know that you are thinking about it within 24 hours or less. Then your hypnotist could make arrangements to keep you under control or keep track of you. Few people can abandon their homes and belongings at a moment's notice, but that is what is required for a successful escape. Don't use credit cards and make phone calls because computers keep track of those things. Don't tell anyone your name and where you are from because they could get in touch with their co-conspirators where you came from and find out how to hypnotize you. If your escape is successful you cannot ever return to any of your former homes. Moses did not return to Egypt until all of the men who knew how to hypnotize him were dead.

CHAPTER 4
CONSPIRATORS AND
NON-CONSPIRATORS

There are conspirators in every family, in every town, in every country in the world. Children are usually brought into a conspiracy by the adult conspirators in their family. Some children are taught to be conspirators from a very early age. For some children the conspirators wait to see if they will get hypnotized. Most who become conspirators have joined by the age of fifteen or sixteen. I have seen elementary school children who had learned Nazi "attitude", and I've seen teenagers become subdued and cautious after joining the Mafia. The conspirators know which children in their family have been hypnotized. They do not ever invite a hypnotized person to join.

A teenager who hasn't been hypnotized apparently must be invited to join before they become an adult and leave home. By the time someone is eighteen or twenty years old they have either been hypnotized or invited to join a conspiracy. Anyone who is invited to join and refuses gets killed. Any adult who isn't a conspirator has been hypnotized without being aware of it.

Hypnotized people are almost always married to conspirators. It is easier to control a hypnotized person if their hypnotist is married to them and living with them. I know of just three marriages between two hypnotized people. One of my hypnotized relatives married a hypnotized person, and another relative had a friend whose parents were both hypnotized. Those marriages ended in divorce. I cannot recall having been married, but I have reason to believe that I was married to a hypnotized girl during the 1970's. Every other

marriage I have seen was either a hypnotized person married to a conspirator, or two conspirators married to each other. Approximately 75% of all marriages are between a hypnotized person and a conspirator, 20% are between two conspirators, and 5% are between two hypnotized people.

You know that you aren't a conspirator. You don't know that about your spouse, you just think you do. If your spouse gets what they want in every important matter, then your spouse is a conspirator. You might not be able to notice it, but other people can. Matt. Ch. 10, vs. 34-36. "Think not that I am come to send peace on earth: I came not to send peace, but a sword. For I am come to set a man at variance against his father, and the daughter against her mother, and the daughter in law against her mother in law. And a man's foes shall be they of his own household."

Practically anybody who is anybody is a conspirator. That means anyone who has a position of respect in the community, anyone who is an expert on any subject, and anyone who has control of anything important.

Politicians at the national level are conspirators. There might be a few non-conspirator politicians at the state or local level, but not very many. Military officers below the rank of Colonel might be honest, but Colonel and above are conspirators. Most law enforcement officers are conspirators, but there are a few honest ones. They get put in front as human shields if there is any shooting, they don't get promoted, they're liable to be scapegoats for other officers' misconduct, and they'll probably retire early. People who control money, such as bankers, business executives, and bureaucrats, are conspirators. Someone who makes a fortune of millions or billions is probably a conspirator. Or if not, the conspirators will find a way to take it away from them. Someone who owns their own business is likely to be a conspirator. Most businesses are established to supply a conspiracy's needs. Competing businesses usually belong to different conspiracies. Celebrities are conspirators. Many performing artists do sex hypnosis jobs and act as spokesmen for their conspiracy. Every public communication is a conspiracy code message: books, magazines, newspapers, radio, movies, television, speeches, sermons, art, pornography, sports and news broadcasts. The people who write it and direct it are conspirators who compose code messages. The people who edit it and publish it are conspirators who decide which message has priority. Almost everyone who has to have a license to practice their profession is a conspirator; not just doctors and lawyers, but also many other licensed professionals. Many different types of knowledge are denied to non-conspirators; primarily scientific and technical knowledge which might expose conspiracy secrets, but also knowledge which might produce wealth and how-to knowledge for do it yourself projects. Everything important is owned, controlled, and done by conspirators. If every conspirator suddenly disappeared, civilization would fall.

But low rank or status isn't proof of honesty. Some businesses and some bureaucracies don't admit that they need security personnel. They use janitors as covert security, and those janitors are conspirators. But some places the janitor is a hypnotized person. There are conspirators at every level of society, but higher levels are more likely to be occupied by conspirators.

There are bound to be exceptions from each of the categories mentioned, and there might be more exceptions from now on, but until I started writing this the vast majority from each category had always been conspirators. If you are an innocent, honest, non-conspirator who happens to be a politician, or high ranking military officer, or doctor, or lawyer, study the personalities of others who have the same type of position. You might learn to recognize conspirators.

Everyone does what a conspiracy wants them to. Conspirators do it knowingly, hypnotized people do it unwittingly. That makes it difficult to decide whether someone is a conspirator judging by what they do. There are just a few revealing acts.

Conspirators don't make the same mistakes over

and over. Conspirators have knowledge and sources of information that hypnotized people don't have. They know who their enemies are without having it explained to them, they know whether something is safe or dangerous, and they're likely to be somewhere else when something bad happens. (If it was planned by their conspiracy, or if it was something that all three conspiracies knew about.)

Conspirators don't have to be hypnotized into doing bad things to people. If they do something obstructive or destructive in a situation that wasn't planned, and a situation where no one could have hypnotized them in response to the unplanned situation, then they were acting on their own initiative so they're a conspirator. But you have to decide whether it was planned based on how they act, because there aren't very many things that can't be planned by a conspiracy.

Most of the time you have to decide whether someone is honest based on how they act. That's quicker, but not completely reliable. So far, just one person that I thought was honest eventually proved to be a conspirator.

Conspirators don't act brainwashed. When someone believes the wrong thing or does the wrong thing, either they are being illogical or they are being dishonest. The illogical person has been hypnotized and the dishonest person is the conspirator who hypnotized them. You can tell the difference.

When conspirators are doing something for their conspiracy, they act differently from how an honest person would act in that situation. Conspirators seem more intelligent because they learn to think to solve problems and hypnotized people don't. The person in your family to whom you would go if you had a question or a problem is probably a conspirator. Conspirators take pleasure in unrighteousness; they enjoy their enemies' misfortune and they enjoy their power. Conspirators smile a smile that says "I know something you don't."

Conspirators don't all have the same type of personality, but they do not often have the type of personality that a hypnotized person has. Some conspirators are cold and calculating. Some are hard and tough. Some are smooth manipulators. Some don't respect hypnotized people. Some feel guilty about being dishonest, and it shows. Some don't believe in right and wrong, and it shows. Most act fakey and dishonest at least part of the time. Once you understand that it comes from being a conspirator, you can recognize conspirators.

CHAPTER 5
DIFFERENCES BETWEEN CONSPIRACIES

Innocent people are often hypnotized first by one conspiracy and then by another. You might be able to tell which conspiracy has you hypnotized by how you feel. Nazi hypnosis is stressful. You are being tortured while you are under hypnosis, and it has an effect on you while you are conscious. You feel sad, unhappy, and depressed, possibly angry, possibly suicidal. Fed hypnosis makes you feel like a robot; dull and emotionless. Mafia hypnosis can cause compulsive masturbation, but otherwise has the least effect on your feelings.

But these symptoms aren't infallible because all three conspiracies use other conspiracies' methods whenever necessary. For the Nazis, pleasure hypnosis is the second choice and Fed hypnosis is the last resort. For the Feds, Nazi hypnosis is the second choice and sex hypnosis is the last resort. For the Mafia, Fed hypnosis is the second choice and Nazi hypnosis is the last resort. I have been hypnotized by all three methods and know that Mafia hypnosis is preferable for the hypnotized person.

Each conspiracy has its own agenda; that's what causes politics and social conflicts. If the people in your family or the people you normally associate with are in favor of unilateral disarmament, in the form of either gun control laws or arms control treaties, they're probably Feds. If your people are in favor of abortion, euthanasia, and doctor assisted suicide, or support causes which imply that people are animals and animals are people, they're probably Nazis. If you know a lady who would like to be able to breastfeed in public, without covering herself with cloth, she's probably Mafia or hypnotized by Mafia.

There are similarities between Nazis and Feds. Both are willing to mass murder everyone who isn't a member of their conspiracy, given the opportunity to do so. Both prefer all-powerful government with people as slaves. Both like to fool people with anti-Christian, anti-reason, paranormal fakery; astrology and psychics from the Feds, flying saucers and the new age movement from the Nazis. They fight each other, but they are natural allies against the Mafia.

Nazis are terrorists. Nazis believe that might makes right. Nazis look for weakness or fear and attack it. Judeo-Christian morality is based on the commandment to love your neighbor as yourself. Nazi ideology is to do bad things to your neighbor because that is how you gain power and enslave them. Nazis justify that by saying that they are the only true human beings. Everyone else is an animal. They have a test to separate the human beings from the animals which I have seen described several different times. The Nazi recruit is required to hold his hand or arm above a flame, or put his hand or arm to something hot, and let it burn him. If he withdraws his hand or arm too soon he is an animal to be hypnotized or killed. See <u>Dune</u>, Kung Fu, Lethal Weapon, Wiseguy, Jungle to Jungle, and others.

The Nazis are the best at rabble rousing, mob psychology, exploiting moral issues, and taking advantage of any disruption of society. If what I say is accepted as truth and causes an upheaval, the Nazis are likely to benefit. If you try to throw the bums out, they might be replaced by worse bums. Nazis love reform movements and witch hunts. They also like to have a strong, fearless leader for everyone to idolize. According to the Bible, the Nazis are going to rule the world, and when they do, it will be similar to Nazi Germany during the 1930's and 1940's; Anti-Christ and then world war and genocide.

Certain types of crimes are usually committed by Nazis. They include terrorist suicide bombers, hijackings, berserkers who commit mass murder and suicide, riots and wilding, kidnapping for ransom, and kidnapping of children to be sacrificed at initiation rituals. Some Nazis eat just a few bites for ceremonial purposes; others routinely dispose of bodies by eating them. Apparently they prefer skinny young children because if they eat an adult with a normal amount of body fat, it makes them fat. But the Feds have a poison to make people fat which they use on the Mafia, so being fat isn't proof of being a Nazi. Nazis hypnotize men into raping Fed and Mafia women. Nazis poison Feds because Feds poison them, but the Feds use secret poisons and the Nazis sometimes use obvious poisons. Nazis like to hypnotize Feds into committing suicide and the Feds retaliate in kind. Feds like for Nazi religious cults to commit mass suicide, or to make it look like they did. Usually when similar crimes or accidents occur in pairs, the first one was Nazis killing Feds and the second was the Fed retaliation. But sometimes the first one was Mafia killing Nazis or Feds. More than two similar crimes or accidents indicate a conspiracy agenda. Nazis aren't opposed to pleasure hypnosis; they just consider it slow and inefficient, and therefore inferior. Drugs, pornography, and prostitution are likely to be from the Nazis instead of the Mafia.

The Feds have been the strongest conspiracy for at least two thousand years. The Feds want to control everything. Power is the ability to destroy, so the Feds actively seek to be prepared to destroy everything. The Feds want everyone to do only what is permitted, so they want to destroy any opportunity to do what isn't permitted. They want to destroy pleasure because their enemies use pleasure against them. For the past few hundred years their top priorities have been alcohol, tobacco, and firearms, but whatever it is *you* like, they'll get around to it eventually. If the Feds ruled the world, everyone's life would be regimented from birth to death. No one would have any freedom of choice or any pleasure; except some high ranking Feds, of course. No one would be able to do anything about it because the Feds are the best at keeping control once they have control.

The Feds do many different things and control many different things secretly. They secretly force consumer products companies to choose between having their products poisoned and having the Feds shut them down. Normal operating procedure for the Feds is to watch for any unusual occurrence of disease, find out what caused it, and use it to poison people. For example: People who live in one county of Texas have a higher than normal incidence of dental cavities and broken bones. It is learned that the drinking water of that area contains fluoride. The human body mistakes fluoride for calcium; it metabolizes fluoride as if it were calcium. That makes a weak spot in a tooth or bone because it has fluoride where it should have calcium. So the Feds say "Fluoride prevents cavities" and put it in toothpaste. Or for example: Birds which nest at a lake in California have a high rate of birth defects. Water which contains selenium drains into that lake. Selenium is teratogenic, which means that it produces monsters. So the Surgeon General determines that consumer products such as alcohol, tobacco, and pet food will henceforth cause birth defects.

Most of the common health problems of modern man are caused by poisons from the Feds; some in consumer products and some administered individually. Most people who die of cancer were poisoned by the Feds; some at random with poisons in consumer products and some individually murdered for a specific reason.

In addition to poisoning consumer products, the Feds also force consumer products companies to produce products that are deliberately made wrong, and keep some products from being made at all. For example: Fads and fashions in rifle cartridges are caused, to some extent, by the fact that at certain times it isn't possible to purchase good ammunition for some rifles or good bullets of some calibers and weights. So hunters switch to a different cartridge. Or for example: The most sensible alternative fuel for automobiles is hydrogen, but the Feds won't allow hydrogen powered automobiles.

There are lots of other examples. *You* know of some products that aren't made right. Some products aren't made right because the Feds don't want you to have the pleasure or the opportunity or the empowerment that those products could provide. Some products aren't made right because the Feds don't want the companies that produce them to be wealthy. But some products are made wrong just to be nasty and make life difficult for ordinary people. It isn't in the best interest of the consumer products company to make them wrong because it's bad for business. It is only in the best interest of the Feds.

The Feds have caused plagues since at least the Middle Ages. Syphilis, the Black Death, smallpox, and the Irish potato famine were plagues caused by the Feds. What do you think biological warfare laboratories are for? Chemical and biological warfare aren't effective against a properly equipped army; they are only effective against civilians. Biological warfare labs are for producing Legionnaire's disease, herpes simplex, Lyme disease, AIDS, Ebola virus, ehrlichiosis, and most other new diseases.

If someone gets AIDS and doesn't die, it isn't because they were infected with a weaker strain of the virus. It is because they are a Fed conspirator who received the vaccine. AIDS is ideally suited to be controlled by quarantine. If it were a naturally occurring disease and no one was using it as a weapon, then by testing everyone for it and quarantining those who have it you could get rid of it. But no one has ever suggested doing that because they know it wouldn't work. The Feds would infect someone who wasn't quarantined to re-start the plague.

The Feds are the best at murdering people, arranging accidents, and using crime against their enemies. They use secret high technology to commit crimes. They use their blinking light device to penetrate enemy conspiracy defenses to murder them. They use Star Wars lasers which produce an invisible beam to cause plane crashes, explosions, and fires. Most plane crashes are caused by the Feds, and in most cases they are in charge of investigating accidents that they caused.

The Feds control international finance and munitions trade because those are necessities for winning wars. The Feds control scientific research because it produces new weapons. The most powerful new weapon is genetic engineering. Soon they won't need to put poisonous additives into consumer products which are ingested. Any biological product, animal or vegetable, can be made carcinogenic or harmful with genetic engineering. Science the Feds think dangerous to themselves they suppress. Science they can use against their enemies they keep secret.

The Feds control the weather. I cannot explain what type of technology is used for that because I haven't ever come across that information. It is probably something they learned during the International Geophysical Year, 1957-1958. They couldn't use it until they put satellites into orbit. The earliest weather control incidents I know of were in 1976.

It should be obvious that weather control can be used as a weapon, and that they must keep it secret to do so. If a lot of their enemies live in an area with forests or brush, that area gets a drought and a fire. If their enemies live in a low-lying area, that area gets a flood. California gets drought, fire, and then a flood to cause mudslides. If an enemy-controlled city is on the coast, it gets a hurricane and poisonous FEMA trailers. If it is inland, it gets a heat wave with a power failure. Farmers and ranchers who are Feds know in advance what the weather will be, and can plan accordingly. Farmers and ranchers who aren't Feds never know what they'll be hit with next.

Weather control is just one technology the Feds are keeping secret, there are others. The Mafia and the Nazis warn each other of capabilities the Feds are developing by mentioning them in science fiction stories and movies.

One of the Feds' favorite techniques is entrapment. Some traps are baited. If someone seems to be offering you something for nothing, suspect a trap. Sometimes if the Feds have an ulterior motive for persecuting or prosecuting an individual, they deliberately trick that individual into committing an offense, either by instruction or by example. If someone asks or advises you to do something, you should first make sure that it is lawful. Just because you see numerous examples of other people doing something without getting into trouble, it doesn't prove that you can do that without getting into trouble. It might be a conspiracy setting a trap. Sometimes the Feds set traps for the innocent opposition by pretending to be in sympathy with them. Some organizations which purport to be against Fed policies may be an attempt to trick those who are against Fed policies into revealing themselves.

The Feds are expert at infiltrating and destroying from within. The Feds persecuted the early Christians, but Christianity continued to grow. So the Feds changed tactics and adopted Christianity as their own religion. By pretending to be Christians and taking over the church they were eventually able to locate and kill all of the early Christians who knew the truth about conspiracies and hypnosis.

The Mafia is the largest conspiracy. Most normal people with a sense of right and wrong should prefer the Mafia because they are the least objectionable conspiracy. But they're also the weakest conspiracy. The Mafia murders people who are evil, murders them one at a time, and usually murders them for a good reason. Mafia philosophy is "To each his own." The problem with that is that it allows things which are destructive of civilized society, such as drug abuse and homosexuality.

The Mafia is in favor of human rights, individual liberties, and freedom of choice because that helps them hypnotize people. The Mafia created the United States, fought for the freedoms you enjoy. They designed the Bill of Rights to keep the government of the United States from becoming all-powerful, unjust, and oppressive. Apparently they failed to foresee that the Supreme Court would destroy the Bill of Rights by misinterpreting it. But the good news is; the United States isn't going to become a totalitarian dictatorship where millions of people die in the concentration camps. The bad news is; you're going to get nuked instead.

CHAPTER 6
ALAS, BABYLON

In 1973 a very intelligent Mafia lady invented a new kind of trick to play on the Feds. The trick would make one man temporarily untouchable because if the Feds or Nazis killed him, the Feds would be forced to nuke the entire country and kill everyone. It would delay the nuclear war while the Feds made preparations they hadn't planned on, including moving valuable technology or duplicating it elsewhere. That would give the Mafia the chance to use their hypnotized person to try to expose the Feds and their poisons. Several different levels of success were possible. Even in the worst case, the Feds would not benefit from winning the nuclear war because they would be forced to destroy the United States instead of conquering it.

The fact that my death is a trigger for nuclear genocide has kept the conspirators from killing me for twenty years. Publication of this will probably trigger the nuclear war eventually even if I'm still alive, but I must refuse to explain why my death will trigger it because the explanation would trigger it immediately.

Shortly after I die the Feds will explode ground-burst cobalt bombs all across the country. The first bombs to explode will be bombs that have been smuggled in and pre-positioned in border towns, seaports, and major international airports all around the periphery of the lower 48 states. When those bombs explode, that will block all avenues of escape. Then two waves of ICBM's from Russia half an hour apart will destroy cities and towns in the interior and lay down fallout patterns across most of the country. There will be survivors in the clear zones between fallout patterns. Federation conspiracy forces from Russia, Canada, and Mexico will search for survivors in order to kill them. Survivors might be attacked by any weapon in the inventory, but most likely by chemical and biological weapons.

If the explosions and fallout don't kill you, Rev. Ch. 18, vs. 22-23 lists activities which will give away your location and bring death upon you.

"The voice of harpers, and musicians, and of pipers, and trumpeters, shall be heard no more at all in thee" because the Feds will use listening devices in Canada and Mexico to triangulate the location of sounds of human origin.

"No craftsman, of whatsoever craft he be, shall be found any more in thee" because craftsmen will trade their products for food and other commodities. The reconnaissance photo analysts will see the pattern of travel to trade with the craftsman. If people keep going to one location, it is because they need something from that location. The Feds will hit that location.

"The sound of a millstone shall be heard no more at all in thee" because even a very small garden can be seen by satellite reconnaissance. Any type of agricultural activity will provoke a lethal response.

"And the light of a candle shall shine no more at all in thee" because animals don't use fire and lights at night, only people do that. Any light at night will reveal your precise location to people who are trying to kill you. If you light a candle or lantern inside your house at night, they won't need to send a plane to drop nerve gas on you; they'll just zap your house with a laser to burn it down.

"The voice of the bridegroom and of the bride shall be heard no more at all in thee" because when people gather into groups for social occasions it will be seen, and it will make it cheaper and easier for the Feds to kill them. If you don't stay spread out, you're going to get a cluster massacre.

Anyone who succeeds in keeping the Feds from killing them will probably starve to death. Anyone who makes it across the border to Canada or Mexico will be picked up by border patrols and taken to a death factory where they will be murdered. To keep them from resisting, they will probably be told that the death factory is a decontamination center. Anyone from outside who wants to go into the United States to find loved ones will be refused permission. If they go in without permission they will not return. The official position will be that the entire country is lethally radioactive, and to prove their lie is good they will kill anyone who threatens to disprove it.

The way to live through the first nuclear war was to stay away from Hiroshima and Nagasaki. The way to live through the second nuclear war is to stay away from the United States. (And possibly some islands and coastal areas.) The way to live through the third nuclear war will be to stay away from cities and military targets, and have food and water stored in your bomb shelter.

You will have to recognize the abomination of desolation as a warning of imminent attack. You might or might not see the abomination of desolation before Russia destroys the United States, but if you do it won't be in the churches and temples. You will see the abomination of desolation before the breakup of world government that causes World War III, and it will be in the churches and temples. Recognizing the abomination of desolation might give you a longer life on earth. Refusing to worship it will give you eternal life.

Trying to tell people about conspiracies and hypnosis usually doesn't do any good. You get killed, the people you tell don't believe you, or if they do believe you, then they get killed. But I'm dead anyway, and if you don't get away from the United States, you're dead anyway, so I might as well try.

CHAPTER 7
PROOF

Proof is defined as evidence which compels the mind to accept the truth of the matter. But for both hypnotized people and conspirators, what you believe is the result of some other influence. Conspirators are taught what to believe when they join a conspiracy. You could give each of a set of identical triplets to a different conspiracy, and one would grow up to be a good Fed, and one would grow up to be a good Nazi, and one would grow up to be a good Mafia conspirator. And none of them would believe that fighting to rule the world is fruitless and self-destructive. Hypnotized people have emotional responses to ideas they have been hypnotized to reject, and conspirators are taught to check with their co-conspirators before accepting any idea, because they have enemies who will lie to them. Conspirators don't think for themselves either. No one in the world decides what to believe based on facts, logic, and rational argument.

It is easier to find evidence of conspiracies than to find evidence of hypnosis. There isn't any physical evidence of hypnosis. That's one of the reasons they have been able to get away with it for thousands of years. An electroencephalograph could prove different brain wave patterns, but first you must be able to hypnotize someone and build an electroencephalograph. Otherwise you have to rely on the experts, and the experts are conspirators who will lie to you.

When someone joins a conspiracy they are shown how hypnosis works, and that proves it to them. I cannot do that, so I will try to prove that conspiracies exist, that they communicate with code, and that much of the code is about hypnosis. I will give an example of how facts can prove that secrets are being kept, a list of stuff the Feds mess with, and a list of conspiracy code. Stuff the Feds mess with is understandable by anyone. Verifying the code will require an effort from you.

In 1983 I saw a TV show called The Trial of Lee Harvey Oswald. Evidence was presented which proved that Oswald did not kill President Kennedy. I've seen that TV show re-played twice since then, and both times the significant evidence had been edited out. I suppose someone else noticed it, and died as a result. The significant evidence was an X-ray photo showing approximately three dozen bullet fragments inside the skull. Diagrams and descriptions were given of a massive head wound five inches across, with bone and scalp blasted outward. The Zapruder film shows blood and brains blasted out. That is the type of wound produced by a high velocity varmint bullet. Oswald had fired low velocity round nose flat base parallel sided full metal jacket bullets, which are usually called solids.

I'm not a terminal ballistics expert. I intended to write explanations of military tumbler bullets, soft points, rotational velocity, the explosive effect from the shock wave of a sonic boom, and round nose solids. Then I looked for a reference to the treaty that banned explosive bullets and found something written by a terminal ballistics expert which wasn't consistent with what I had said about military tumblers. So I better not pretend to be an expert because an expert could easily prove me wrong about some minor detail.

But I've seen deer killed with low, medium, and high velocity soft point bullets of several different calibers, and I've hunted fur-bearing animals with low velocity round nose solids. I know from personal experience that if you hit a coyote in the head with a low velocity solid, the head will not explode, and the bullet will make small holes entering and exiting. I haven't ever shot a coyote in the head with a high velocity varmint bullet, but I know that high velocity varmint bullets produce an explosive effect, and lots of bullet fragments. I know that terminal ballistic performance is governed by the laws of physics. You will get the same results with each shot if the rifling twist is the same, and the muzzle velocity is the same, and the bullet construction is the same, and the target medium is the same. If you get different results, one or more of those factors wasn't the same. The terminal ballistic performance of the bullet that hit President Kennedy's head was completely different from the terminal ballistic performance of the first two bullets.

Bullets either use their energy to penetrate, or to

produce hydraulic effects, or both. Penetration and hydrostatic shock are normally in inverse proportion. Bullets which penetrate more deeply produce less hydrostatic shock. Bullets which produce more hydrostatic shock penetrate less deeply. Solids are at one end of the performance spectrum where a bullet penetrates deeply because it doesn't produce hydrostatic shock. The bullet that hit President Kennedy's head was at the opposite end of the performance spectrum where a bullet disintegrates on impact and expends all of its energy as hydrostatic shock.

The bullet that hit President Kennedy's head was a high velocity varmint bullet. Anyone who says it was a low velocity solid either doesn't know anything at all about terminal ballistics, or has been hypnotized into believing a lie, or is lying.

There was another rifleman at Dealey Plaza. Once you know there was another rifleman, it's obvious where he fired from. It is easiest to hit a moving target with a rifle if it is moving straight toward you or straight away from you. If it is moving at an angle the rifleman must shoot slightly in front of it, and it is difficult to calculate how far in front of it. At Dealey Plaza the curves of Elm Street gave a straight away shot to riflemen in two different buildings. Elm Street curves and for a short distance runs straight away from the Dal-Tex building, on the northeast corner of the intersection of Elm & Houston. Then after another curve it runs straight toward the triple underpass, straight away from a different building on the east side of Houston. The third shot was fired by a second rifleman in the Dal-

Tex building. If the third shot had missed there would have been a fourth shot from a third rifleman just before the car went under the triple underpass. The Mafia chose to shoot President Kennedy at Dealey Plaza rather than somewhere else because the shape of the street and the placement of the buildings gave so many chances to make an easy shot.

Page 33 of the report of the Warren Commission has an aerial photograph of Dealey Plaza taken from a vantage point which lines up the section of street where President Kennedy was shot with the Dal-Tex building. Whoever chose to use that photograph was making it quite clear that they knew where the third shot was fired from.

The Feds have successfully covered this up for 44 years. They took control of the investigation because they wanted to cover up what the investigation was supposed to be looking for. They had to do several different things to cover it up.

1. They had to keep anyone else from doing the autopsy. The Mafia had counted on the fact that the murder was subject to local jurisdiction, but the Feds took jurisdiction away from them unlawfully and then changed the law to keep that situation from occurring again. The body was unlawfully removed from Dallas without an autopsy despite protests from local officials. The report doesn't say who the officials were or how they lost the argument.

2. They had to keep anyone else from making an expert examination of the bullet fragments from the head wound. The autopsy report states that two bullet fragments, measuring 7 X 2 mm and 3 X 1 mm,

were removed from the right cerebral cortex and given to two F.B.I. agents; Francis X. O'Neill, Jr., and James W. Siebert.

There are a couple of hints in the report that those bullet fragments were from a .257 caliber bullet. Page 554 says that a 6.5mm weapon corresponds to an American .257 caliber. That isn't true. 6.5mm is .264 caliber. They'd probably have corrected such an obvious error if it had been accidental. If it wasn't accidental, then it's probably code. They were saying that the head wound bullet was a .257 caliber bullet. That idea is supported by the fact that they tested three different types of ammunition for shock and penetration, one of which was .257 caliber.

They tested Oswald's 6.5mm 160 grain solids, NATO ball M80, which is a .308 caliber 146 grain military tumbler, and an unspecified weight of soft point bullet fired from a rifle chambered for the .257 Roberts cartridge. The report said ".257 Roberts Winchester", but the .257 Roberts was standardized by Remington, so Winchester probably referred to the ammunition. The .257 Roberts can fire an 87 grain bullet at 3100-3200 fps, or a 100 grain bullet at 2900-3000 fps, or a 117 grain bullet at 2600-2700 fps. If fired from a barrel with a standard rifling twist rate, only the 87 grain bullet would have a rotational velocity high enough to produce an explosive effect. Oswald's solids had an average muzzle velocity of 2165 fps.

The Feds used ballistic gelatin for those tests, but you can re-create the tests by firing the bullets into stacks of water-soaked paper. Fire round nose solids with a muzzle velocity of 2100 or 2200 fps and soft point bullets with a muzzle velocity of 3100 or 3200 fps into stacks of soaked paper at 90 yards. Provided that they are properly constructed, the two bullet types will perform differently after impact. That should prove to any reasonable person that Oswald did not fire the third shot.

The third reason for believing that the head wound bullet was a .257 caliber bullet comes from another murder. A Federal judge named John Wood was shot to death in Dallas during the 1980's. A man named Harrelson was convicted of shooting Judge Wood with a .257 Weatherby Magnum. I believe that the head wound bullet was a 100 grain bullet which had been pulled from a Winchester brand factory loaded .257 Roberts cartridge and then handloaded into a .257 Weatherby Magnum cartridge. Firing the 100 grain bullet at 3300- 3500 fps from the magnum rifle gave it the terminal ballistic performance of a varmint bullet.

The forward portion of the bullet jacket peeled back into a mushroom shape. The forward portion of the lead core disintegrated into small fragments. Several different forces (some of which I don't understand completely because I'm not an expert) pulled the core forward and separated it from the jacket. The jacket stopped penetrating immediately after the core separated. The core penetrated only slightly farther because most of the bullet's energy had been expended as hydrostatic shock. The two bullet fragments which were removed from the brain and given to the F.B.I. agents were probably the base of the bullet jacket and the largest fragment of the lead core.

If those bullet fragments still exist, they are the proof that the Federal government deliberately lied. Anyone familiar with different bullet types could look at the bullet jacket and see immediately that it was the jacket of a soft point bullet instead of a solid. To determine the bullet diameter and which lot of ammunition the bullet came from would require examination by experts. The experts would have to be Nazi or Mafia conspirators willing to give an honest report despite knowing that the Feds would kill them for it.

3. They had to rig tests to falsely re-create the head wound with low velocity solids. They had to keep saying that Oswald's ammunition could cause the head wound, and they needed support for that position.

Tests were performed at Edgewood Arsenal, Maryland under the supervision of Dr. Alfred G. Olivier. 10 shots were fired at "reconstructed inert" human skulls filled with ballistic gelatin. The report says that one of those 10 shots blew out the side of the skull and produced two bullet fragments similar to the large fragments found in the Presidential limousine. (The fragments found in the Presidential limousine, weighing 44.6 and 21 grains, were actually from the neck wound bullet.)

If there were independent observers present at the tests, the Feds could have used a bullet which was deliberately constructed improperly, or used a bullet which contained an explosive charge to blow it apart in the middle. Explosive bullets were banned by treaty long ago but could still be built. If there weren't any independent observers at the tests, the Feds could simply have lied.

Dr. Olivier's comments about the tests are quoted in the report. "It disclosed that the type of head wounds that the President received could be done by this type of bullet. This surprised me very much, because this type of stable bullet I didn't think would cause a massive head wound, I thought it would go through making a small entrance and exit, but the bones of the skull are enough to deform the end of this bullet causing it to expend a lot of energy and blowing out the side of the skull or blowing out fragments of the skull."

That seems as if the Feds neglected to agree on the story they would tell. Did the end of the bullet deform, or did it break apart in the middle? It isn't very likely that both would happen.

Even if the bullet deformed the velocity wasn't high enough to produce an explosive effect. To produce explosive hydrostatic shock with bullets fired from a barrel having a twist rate of one turn in 10 inches the muzzle velocity must be above 3100 fps. Oswald's rifle had a faster twist rate than that, but not fast enough to produce an explosive effect at muzzle velocities below 2800 fps. Oswald's solids had a muzzle velocity 600 fps below the muzzle velocity required, by the laws of physics, to produce an explosive effect.

Even if the bullet broke in two it would not have left so many fragments in the skull. Two or three fragments: certainly. Half a dozen or a dozen: possibly. Three dozen: impossible. The explosive effect and the large number of bullet fragments could only have been produced by a high velocity soft point bullet.

4. They had to ignore the possibility that shots might have been fired from any of the buildings on the east side of Houston Street. The only areas the Warren Commission investigated as a possible source of the shots were the school book depository building, the railroad yards, and the triple underpass. That is not a thorough and impartial investigation. They do not mention any witnesses who said that they heard shots fired from anywhere else. Even if Oswald had fired all three shots there would have been a few confused witnesses who thought the shots came from the wrong side of Houston Street. If that had been the case the Warren Commission would have reported that witnesses thought they heard shots from the east side of Houston Street and explained how they investigated and found that the witnesses were wrong. They failed to do so because that's what they were covering up.

5. They had to kill everyone who had heard the shot fired from the Dal-Tex building. I've heard rumors about the fact that most of the people who witnessed the assassination died during the next few years. I haven't read any of those stories. You might read them to find out how many different ways a conspiracy can arrange to kill someone.

6. They had to kill Oswald. The Mafia planned to use Oswald to expose Fed hypnosis and start a nuclear war with Russia. If Oswald had stood trial they would have proved that he was hypnotized while in Russia and the Russians used him as a hypnotized murderer, just as in <u>The Manchurian</u>

Candidate. During interrogation Oswald denied purchasing a rifle, having his picture taken with the rifle, bringing the rifle to the depository building, and knowing anything of the shooting of President Kennedy or the shooting of Tippit. He didn't remember those things because they happened while he was under hypnosis. The Mafia would have made a public demonstration of hypnotizing Oswald into recalling the assassination as part of their plan to expose Fed hypnosis. Then Oswald would have remembered firing the first two shots but denied firing the third shot. The fact that another rifleman fired from the Dal-Tex building would have been exposed. The Mafia must have had evidence planted to establish a connection between the rifleman in the Dal-Tex building and Russia. Most innocent people would have believed that the Russians murdered President Kennedy. There would have been a nuclear war which the United States would have won. The Feds did whatever was necessary to keep that from happening.

The Mafia knew that the Feds were planning for Russia to win a nuclear war and made several attempts to start the nuclear war while the United States could still win it. The Cuban missile crisis and the assassination of President Kennedy were Mafia attempts to start a war. There may have been other attempts which were blocked without any publicity. Warnings to the Feds may have included No Blade of Grass, Alas, Babylon, Fail-Safe, The Quiller Memorandum, and Doctor Strangelove.

The Mafia probably had several different reasons to assassinate President Kennedy. They said that he was wanted for treason. I suspect that that means he was originally Mafia and defected to another conspiracy, but it could mean that he had a deal with the Mafia and broke it. I've heard that he was expected to commit the United States to the Mafia program of building bomb shelters but instead committed us to the Fed program to put a man on the moon. He did what the Feds wanted done to checkmate the Cuban missile crisis. His administration adopted the unconstitutional, illogical, and immoral doctrine of Mutual Assured Destruction, which says that we must not defend ourselves because it would upset the balance of power. That allows the Russians to upset the balance of power to their advantage. The Mafia was using a tactic of killing two birds with one stone. Kill one enemy and blame it on another enemy and attack them too.

I have said that Russia will destroy the United States shortly after I die. If that happens as predicted, it cannot be dismissed as coincidence. My view of reality will have been proven correct. If I'm right about nuclear war, then I'm probably right about conspiracies and hypnosis. How else could I have known? I'm not a prophet. God hasn't told me to tell you anything. It's just that I found out what the conspirators know, and lived long enough to explain it to innocent people. But everyone in the United States who refuses to believe me will be killed by the nuclear war. I'm trying to save your life, and you're going to repay me by thinking I'm crazy. Those who are intelligent enough to realize that nuclear war is a real possibility and tough enough to make the difficult decision to leave the

United States will find out I'm not crazy. The nuclear war should prove to you that you have been hypnotized without your knowledge and consent, and that conspiracies are fighting to rule the world.

Bible prophecy foretells the results of the fight to rule the world. If Bible prophecy comes true, then the Bible is the word of God.

CHAPTER 8
STUFF THE FEDS MESS WITH

Part A: Stuff Poisoned by the Feds

Combination Poisons
1. A college English textbook with examples of exposition which was in use during the early 1970's said that the combination of ingredients for baked beans was poisonous.
2. Mystery novels by a bestselling author warning of combination poisons: In 1964 the Feds poisoned the combination of fried chicken with sweet corn and pineapple and bacon. In 1974 they poisoned beer and Coke. In 1976 they poisoned brandy and ginger ale. In 1981 they poisoned ham and tomatoes and brown toast. In 1984 they poisoned cornflakes and toast. In 1988 they poisoned Burgundy and beef sandwiches.
3. A crime drama that was on TV in 1989 said that the combination of beer and a snack was poisonous. The code was a hand signal given by one of the actors.
4. A book about archery which was published in 1989 said that the combination of beer and potato

salad was poisonous.

I'll take a wild guess that there are some other things which are poisonous in combination with beer.

5. Sometime between 2000 and 2004 I got an idea that the combination of sugar and cinnamon was poisonous, but I can't remember what made me think so. If it's true, then you cannot make cinnamon toast and apple pie at home.

Stuff That Is Poisonous by Itself

1. I heard someone in the media say that if you want to stop biting your fingernails, put vanilla extract or almond extract on your fingernails. I'll take a wild guess that that will stop you from biting your fingernails one way or another because they're poisonous. If it's true, then you must leave the vanilla out of a lot of different types of sweets, and you cannot make pancake syrup.

2. In 1990 U.S. military MRE's (Meals Ready to Eat) were poisonous, but not necessarily lethal. Gulf War Syndrome was caused by various poisons in the MRE's. Different MRE meals contained different poisons, and the different poisons produced different ailments. The fact that Gulf War Syndrome wasn't just one type of ailment allowed the Federal government to say that Gulf War Syndrome doesn't exist. They poisoned our soldiers and then refused to admit that their ailments were connected to their Gulf War service. Soldiers who asked for food from home, and people who sent it, knew about the MRE's. I didn't learn this from code, just from several different reports of soldiers refusing to eat the

MRE's, and remembering how they acted on TV asking for food. The reason the Feds poisoned the MRE's is that they expected them to be eaten by U.S. soldiers who were fighting against a Russian invasion in 1990. But the Mafia played a dirty trick which delayed and escalated the war.

3. Two movies during the 1970's said that camera flashbulbs emit harmful radiation. That's why cameras switched from flashbulbs to electronic flash.

4. During the 1970's the Feds poisoned wood stocks for bolt action rifles. During the 1980's they also poisoned the factory stocks of the Ruger Ranch Rifle. That created a demand for aftermarket stocks, which at first were made of fiberglass and then of plastic. The excuse conspirators gave for switching to fiberglass stocks was that wood stocks can absorb water, which makes them swell up and warp, affecting accuracy, but the real reason was that the Feds were poisoning wood stocks. Wood stocks which are properly cared for don't warp unless somebody messes with them. (That's also true of self bows made of properly seasoned wood.) I think the Feds stopped poisoning rifle stocks during the 1990's, but I'm not sure.

5. During the 1980's the Feds poisoned breast implants, but I think they stopped poisoning them during the 1990's.

6. I think the reason that a lot of married couples have decided that contraceptives are immoral during the last few years is that the Feds are poisoning contraceptives. Probably not all of them are poisonous, but you have to be careful, and the Feds could switch non-poisonous for poisonous if you use

them. Actually, abortion is immoral but contraception isn't.

7. Someone gave me a code signal at the supermarket that paper towels are poisonous, but I don't know whether they all are, or just the brand I ordinarily buy.

8. Mystery novels by a bestselling author warning of stuff that had been poisoned: In 1971 the Feds stopped poisoning turkey sandwiches. In 1978 they poisoned milk. (A movie said so too.) In 1982 they poisoned salami. In 1984 they poisoned plastic raincoats. In 1985 they poisoned wine made in California. (A TV commercial said so too.) In 1992 they poisoned chocolate cake.

9. Several different motion sickness remedies have come into use and then gone out of use during the past thirty or forty years, probably because the Feds poison them.

10. The Feds poison lick-to-moisten glue on envelopes and stamps. That's why the U. S. Postal Service started issuing peel & stick stamps. But they don't poison the glue of every brand of envelopes all the time. Envelopes made by Feds might be safe.

11. Ordinary table salt is supposed to be sodium chloride. The Feds found a chemical called lithium chloride which looks and tastes exactly like salt. But lithium chloride causes high blood pressure and strokes. So the Feds used their big lie technique. They lied by saying that salt causes high blood pressure and strokes and then made the lie come true by poisoning table salt with lithium chloride. But they don't poison every brand of salt all the time. Salt is a necessary nutrient for Feds as well as

everyone else. They're more likely to slip poisoned salt to someone they don't like.

12. For a while the Feds poisoned Danforth anchors to force everyone to use plow anchors, but I don't know when they started poisoning them and when they stopped. Bob Stearns wrote an article about a similar anchor which could be homemade. He said they wouldn't patent it. The reason they didn't want to patent it and put it into commercial production is that the Feds would have messed with it. Apparently the Feds don't like lightweight anchors.

What type of food did you stop eating which you used to eat? Most often the real reason is that the Feds poisoned it. Can you recollect and understand why you switched to a different type of food?

Part B: Stuff the Feds Mess With

1. <u>Aluminum.</u> The Feds mess with almost anything made of aluminum except cookware and some powerboats and airplanes. Anything which could be made either of aluminum or fiberglass, the Feds want it made of fiberglass. Examples are boats and tent poles. Anything which could be made either of aluminum or steel, the Feds want it made of steel. Examples are food cans, garbage cans, and lids on glass jars. There are probably several different reasons why the Feds don't want people to have good stuff made of aluminum. Aluminum production and manufacturing are probably controlled by a different conspiracy. Feds probably control production of glass, fiberglass, steel, and oil. Aluminum doesn't corrode from any natural environmental influence

and it doesn't wear out from anything except flexing and vibration fatigue. So aluminum products last longer and are more cost effective- it's cheaper in the long run. The Feds don't want you to have something that will last a lifetime; they want you to have to buy a new one every five or ten years. They are especially opposed to aluminum sailboats and canoes. It was possible to buy good aluminum canoes during the 1960's and 1970's, but during the 1990's I talked to a boat dealer who said that aluminum canoes were no-good; the rivets loosened and made them leak. There isn't any reason for that to happen unless somebody is messing with them. There aren't any mass-produced aluminum sailboats, neither trailer-sailers nor cruisers, because the Feds won't allow it. They only allow large, expensive, custom-built aluminum sailboats for wealthy people. If you are wealthy enough to hire a naval architect to design it and a boatshop to build it, they'll allow that.

2. <u>Sloops.</u> If you read a book or magazine article written by Feds between 1986 and 2004 and it talks about a junk rig for a sailboat, it is code for a sloop rig. The word junk is code which means they poisoned it or messed with it. I learned this from a magazine article. I had decided to build a ferrocement boat with a sloop rig, and then I read the magazine article. It was supposed to be talking about someone else, but it said he built a ferrocement boat with a junk rig. So I figured out that it was talking about me and junk rig meant sloop rig. The Feds control the weather, so they can make the wind blow against you when you try to sail some-

where. If you have a sloop rig you can sail against the wind and get there, even though it will take twice as long. But if you have a ketch rig it doesn't sail against the wind as well and it will take you three times as long to get there. So the Feds want you to have a ketch rig instead of a sloop rig, so they mess with sloop rigged sailboats.

3. Inexpensive boat fittings. The Feds don't want people to build their own sailboat unless it is made of fiberglass. They mess with bronze screws used for conventional plank-on-frame sailboat construction. You could get good bronze screws at a hardware store up until the 1970's, but by the 1980's if you tried to use a bronze screw the head of the screw would twist off. You can't get good turnbuckles at a hardware store either. They are deliberately made flimsy to fail under strain. The fact that you couldn't get good screws led to the use of ring-shanked nails and stitch-and-glue joints. The lack of good turnbuckles has led to the use of primitive lashings for small sailboat rigging.

4. Flashlights and bulbs. Between 1992 and 2002 every flashlight I bought which had a conventional on/off switch developed an annoying habit of turning itself off when it was supposed to be on. I used flashlights belonging to my relatives and they did the same thing. That led to flashlights which turn on and off by screwing and unscrewing the bulb housing, the first example of which was Maglite. But the Feds invented a way to mess with Maglites too. The first Mini Maglite I had worked very well and lasted a long time. The next one had a problem with the bulb burning out. The bulb burned out after just a

couple of weeks, and I purchased and installed a new bulb, and it burned out after a couple of weeks, and I put in a new bulb and it burned out. So after three or four bulbs I figured out there was something wrong with it and quit using it. Apparently the Feds don't like Maglite. And the latest thing is using light-emitting diodes instead of bulbs. That's probably a good idea for traffic lights, but the modern bulbs used by Maglite and some others put out brighter light and are preferable for flashlights.

5. <u>Toilets.</u> The Feds passed a law that every new toilet installed after a certain date had to be a new design which used a smaller amount of water to flush. Then they messed with the new toilets so that they would not flush properly. You had to flush them several times to get stuff to flush, which defeated the intention of saving water. And that was just to be nasty; there isn't any justification for it, even by Fed ideology.

6. <u>Emission tests.</u> The Federal government mandates exhaust emission tests for cars in urban areas that suffer from air pollution. If someone who is Mafia takes their car in to be tested, the Nazis and Feds who do the testing can arrange for the test to damage that car. But pickup trucks and SUV's are exempt from the tests, so everybody who lives in those areas drives either a pickup or an SUV to avoid the tests. Since I first wrote this I've heard spin control about it in the media. They said that pickups and SUV's give better protection in a crash. So that gives conspirators an excuse they can use; they don't drive an SUV to avoid the tests, they drive an SUV because it gives them better surviv-

ability if they have a wreck. It is quite common for conspirators to lie about the real reasons they avoid some things and prefer others. And the correct solution to air pollution is hydrogen powered automobiles, because the exhaust from a hydrogen engine is just ordinary water vapor. The water vapor can be recycled and turned into fuel, so you aren't ever going to have fuel shortages with hydrogen. Anywhere you have water and electricity you can make hydrogen. That's why the Feds are against it; because they couldn't control the fuel supply. So they don't allow hydrogen powered engines. The safety problem was solved years ago by a substance which absorbs hydrogen gas and releases it slowly, preventing explosions.

7. <u>Wheelbarrows</u>. The only wheelbarrows you can buy are deliberately made wrong. They have wooden handles which can splinter and break that are too close together. The bin is too narrow and too tall, which gives too high a center of gravity. The wheel has a pneumatic rubber tire. They are deliberately made to tip over too easily, and be completely useless when the tire goes flat. If you want to see how wheelbarrows should be made, look at some old Southern Pacific Railroad wheelbarrows. Every part is made of steel, including the wagon wheel type wheel. The handles are made of steel pipe, far enough apart to give stability. The bin is low and flat to give a low center of gravity. They don't tip over and the tires cannot go flat. You could make a wheelbarrow like the railroad wheelbarrows with the bin made of aluminum and the other parts made of stainless steel, and it would last

for several hundred years, or until it was accidentally damaged. But that's assuming it was made right, with stainless steel which really wouldn't rust. It would be expensive but it would be cheaper in the long run.

8. <u>Garbage cans.</u> During the 1970's and 1980's galvanized steel garbage cans kept getting smaller and flimsier and during the 1990's they disappeared from the stores. No one was selling metal garbage cans because no one was buying them because they were no-good. Everyone bought plastic garbage cans instead. The last one I bought has a label on it which says that it should not be used for other than its intended purpose. That explains why the Feds messed with them. Those metal garbage cans could be used as rat-proof containers for storing food in bulk. The Feds don't want you to do that, so they poisoned them, so everybody stopped buying them. But those steel garbage cans rust and get holes in them within a few years. It should have been obvious years ago that it would be better to make them of aluminum, but the Feds don't want you to have that.

9. <u>Tarps.</u> You cannot buy a good tarp anymore.

10. <u>The Hubble space telescope.</u> They deliberately made the mirrors wrong.

11. <u>Drags of fishing reels.</u> Good quality spinning reels which were made during the 1980's had Teflon drag washers. Teflon has a smooth, non-stick surface and it resists heat. That gives you a smooth drag which can apply a lot of braking pressure for a long time without being damaged by the heat produced. So the Feds started forcing the reel manufac-

turers to use poorer quality felt drag washers during the 1990's. The reels were redesigned so the old drag washers wouldn't fit the new reel spools. For a while they allowed Teflon drag washers in no-good poisoned reels, so people took the Teflon washers out of the no-good reels to put them into good reels. I read some code about it in a mail order catalog, telling conspirators that a certain brand of reels was no-good but they had good drag washers. There may have been other sources of Teflon too. So it was too easy for people to get Teflon washers for their reels. So what did the Feds do? They used their big lie technique. They started saying that Teflon was carcinogenic and should be banned. I haven't heard whether they actually did ban the manufacture of Teflon, but if they did, it isn't because it's bad for you. It's because it makes good drag washers, and they don't want you to have that.

12. <u>Beaters of electric mixers.</u> Recently I've seen beaters of electric mixers made in an unconventional shape. The conventional shape is just as wide at the bottom as at the top. The no-good ones are narrower at the bottom than at the top. That reduces the angular velocity at the bottom where it is doing the mixing, so you have to use a higher speed to get it to mix as well. The old time hand-cranked mixers had beaters which were wider at the bottom than at the top. That is probably the best shape for beaters. The no-good beaters have it reversed; upside down. But I saw the no-good beaters after I started writing this, so if no one else has ever seen those no-good beaters, then the conspiracy was setting me up to look crazy.

13. <u>Box fans.</u> During the mid to late 1990's box fans started to be made with fan blades of a new design which wouldn't create a breeze. That's an example of new & improved means no-good. The fan blade attachment was redesigned to keep people from putting good fan blades from the old fans onto the new fans. Recently I've seen box fans that are only about half the normal thickness from front to back. That means they won't stand up by themselves like a box fan should.

14. <u>Baseball cap headband fasteners.</u> Baseball caps suddenly began to be made with Velcro fasteners and strap & buckle fasteners after I started writing this. Apparently for years the Feds had been forcing the baseball cap manufacturers to use those hole & pintle plastic fasteners.

15. <u>Camping stoves?</u> I bought an inexpensive camp stove and it was no-good, has anyone else had that experience? Maybe the most expensive ones work properly. Maybe Fed conspirators can get good camp stoves but no one else can. I know they do that with other stuff.

16. <u>Timepiece accuracy.</u> Digital watches are deliberately made to be less accurate than they could be. They ought to be accurate to within a few seconds per year but instead they're accurate to a few seconds per week. That's why the technology of resetting timepieces automatically with radio signals was invented. It's a Rube Goldberg solution to a problem that shouldn't exist.

17. <u>Bowstrings.</u> Dacron bowstrings made before the 1990's weren't stretchy. During the 1990's the Feds started forcing Dacron bowstrings to be made

stretchy, so everybody switched to a new type of bowstring.

18. <u>Rifles.</u> European nations began equipping their armies with bolt action rifles during the 1880's. The Germans adopted the 8X57mm cartridge and a bolt action rifle for it in 1888. The British adopted the .303 cartridge and a bolt action rifle for it in 1888-1889. The French Lebel may have been earlier. Except possibly for the Lebel, all of the early military bolt action rifles were designed to fire round nose flat base parallel sided full metal jacket bullets with a long length and a high sectional density. That's exactly the same kind of bullet Oswald fired from his 6.5X52mm Mannlicher-Carcano Italian Model 91. A fast rifling twist is required to stabilize those bullets for accuracy. Someone named Greenhill invented a formula for calculating the proper rifling twist. The Greenhill formula states that the bullet length expressed as calibers multiplied by the rifling twist expressed as calibers per turn should equal 150. As rifles became more efficient, bullet diameters decreased and the rifling twists increased.

I don't know why they used round nose solids. Those bullets had a slightly higher muzzle velocity than larger caliber blackpowder cartridge bullets, they retained velocity downrange better, and they penetrated better. Until those round nose solid bullets were invented it was practically impossible to kill elephant and rhino with a rifle. But better penetration doesn't give greater killing power with a lung shot. The British soon discovered that their .303 bolt action rifles did not kill the enemy tribesmen they were fighting as quickly as the .45 caliber single shot rifles they had used previously. The bullet would drill a small hole through one lung and the enemy tribesman would not fall down and die until both lungs had collapsed or filled with blood, which might take anywhere up to twenty minutes to happen. British soldiers in the field began altering the bullets by hand to turn them into soft point mushrooming bullets which would kill more quickly. Usually they cut an X through the bullet jacket at the nose. Bullets which had been altered in that manner were called dum-dum bullets. Some countries, such as Argentina, used explosive bullets. But in the late 1800's an international treaty banned the use of explosive bullets and soft point bullets for warfare. That was hypocrisy. The purpose of shooting an enemy soldier with a rifle is to kill him, and the quicker it kills him the better. But some people attempted to prove moral superiority by pretending to be horrified at the thought of the wounds inflicted by frangible bullets. That has been a favorite type of propaganda for the Feds ever since. They always call soft point bullets dum-dum bullets. There are two ways to see that that is a misnomer. The first way is that no one alters round nose solids any more, so there aren't any dum-dum bullets. The second way is that every bullet, whether it is a civilian soft point or a military tumbler, is a frangible bullet, so every bullet is a dum-dum bullet. Round nose solids aren't used for anything except hunting elephant and rhino, or for plinking, and most other types of rifle bullets are special purpose military bullets. 90% of all rifle bullets fired since World War II have been frangible bullets. Calling a bullet a dum-dum bullet these days is a propaganda ploy intended to provoke an emotional response from uninformed people. (It might be code, too.)

The United States Army adopted the .30-40 cartridge and the Krag bolt action rifle in 1893. The .30-40 fired a 220 grain .308 caliber round nose solid. The muzzle velocity was probably in the vicinity of 1900 or 2000 fps. During the Spanish-American war the 220 grain solids were found to lack killing power and the Krag rifle was found to be less than perfect. The Spanish 1893 Mauser rifle and its 7X57mm cartridge were clearly superior. Many people wanted the U.S. Army to adopt a Mauser rifle chambered for 7X57mm, but the Feds wouldn't allow it. From 1893 to 1963 the Feds in the United States insisted that the army use .30 caliber cartridges, probably because of the code meaning of 30 and 308. In 1903 the U.S. Army adopted an improved rifle chambered for a larger .30 caliber cartridge, called the .30-'03. It fired the same 220 grain solid at a slightly higher velocity; 2300 fps. That did not increase killing power because the problem was the type of bullet used.

Then the Germans discovered that full metal jacket bullets of a shorter length having a sharp conical point would tumble and turn base forward very quickly after impacting flesh. When they turned base forward, the base of the bullet, which had the lead core exposed, would mushroom and fragment. Those spitzer tumbler bullets complied with the treaty requirement for a full metal jacket bullet, but gave the killing power of a soft point bullet. The Germans switched from 227 grain .318

caliber round nose solids to 154 grain .323 caliber spitzer tumblers in 1905.

The U.S. Army decided to adopt a .30 caliber spitzer tumbler bullet which weighed 150 grains. That was stupid. If they wanted to duplicate the terminal ballistic performance of the German bullet they should have duplicated its sectional density, muzzle velocity, and rotational velocity. They probably wanted to ensure that their bullet would retain velocity, and therefore accuracy, farther downrange than the German bullet. But that isn't sensible either because the average infantryman and infantry rifle aren't accurate enough to hit an enemy soldier past 600 yards.

The 150 grain bullet could have been fired from the .30-'03 cartridge in the 1903 Springfield rifles, but it would have been inaccurate. If the 150 grain bullet were fired in a chamber designed to accommodate the 220 grain bullet seated out full length, it would have too much free travel before engaging the rifling. It would enter the bore tipped slightly sideways, which would cause poor accuracy. That problem occurs with all of the early military bolt action rifles which were intended for use with high sectional density solids, such as the 7X57mm and most of the early 6.5mm cartridges, including the 6.5X52mm. But the Feds have always lied and said that the fast rifling twist of the 7mm and 6.5mm barrels causes the lighter weight spitzer bullets to be inaccurate. It isn't the rifling twist; it's the length of the throat of the chamber. The Feds knew that, so they re-chambered the 1903 rifles to shorten the throat of the chamber. To give themselves an excuse for re-chambering the rifles, they shortened the .30-'03 case by .07" and called it the .30-'06. That allowed them to conceal the real reason for re-chambering the rifles. They could say that the rifles were being re-chambered for the .30-'06 cartridge without mentioning that they were shortening the throat of the chamber.

Wildcat is a term which refers to non-standard cartridges which handloaders make by altering another cartridge case, usually by necking it down or necking it up. The term originated from the practice of necking down larger caliber cases to fire smaller caliber bullets at higher velocity for the purpose of shooting varmints such as wildcats. (But it probably has a code meaning, too.) Of the cartridges standardized during the first 75 years of the twentieth century, approximately 15% were designed for military use, 56% were designed by commercial firms for civilian use, and 28% originated as wildcats. When wildcat cartridges become very popular, the arms and ammunition manufacturers standardize them as factory loaded cartridges, provided that the Feds allow it.

Wildcatters learned that the .30-'06 case could be made into a more efficient cartridge having greater killing power by necking it down. A 7mm-'06 wildcat firing a 140 grain bullet from the faster twist of the 7mm barrel would zap an elk (wapiti) dead in its tracks with a lung shot. So would a 6.5mm-'06 wildcat firing a 120 grain bullet. The .30-'06 wouldn't. The reason is that the faster twist of the smaller caliber barrels would give a bullet with a sectional density of .247 a rotational velocity high enough to produce an explosive shock wave. The slower twist of the .30 caliber barrel wouldn't do that with a bullet having a sectional density of .225. Faster rifling twists produce the explosive shock wave at a lower muzzle velocity. The explosive shock wave phenomenon was something completely new. It wasn't possible until jacketed bullets, smokeless powders, and bolt action rifles made high velocity possible. The Feds decided they didn't like it and wouldn't allow it. They wouldn't allow commercial production of standardized 7mm-'06 and 6.5mm-'06 rifles in the U.S. For many years 140 grain 7mm bullets and 120 grain 6.5mm bullets were deliberately made wrong to keep wild-catters from zapping elk dead.

The British standardized a cartridge similar to a 7mm-'06 called the .280 Ross sometime prior to 1910. The Germans standardized a cartridge similar to a 7mm-'06 called the 7X64mm Brenneke in 1917. In the United States the 7mm-'06 wasn't standardized until 1957. The reason the Feds finally allowed it was the development of 7mm magnum cartridges such as the 7mm Weatherby Magnum (1944) and the 7X61 Sharpe & Hart (1953) which would zap an elk dead using bullets heavier than 140 grains. The 7mm-'06 was standardized as the .280 Remington, but it had too slow a twist. The rifling twist for any 7mm cartridge should be between one turn in 8.6" (the original twist for the 7X57mm) and one turn in 9" (the slowest which will stabilize a 175 grain spitzer boattail.) The .280 was standardized with a twist of one turn in 9.25". The slower twist and the bad bullets kept it from zapping elk dead.

The .270 Winchester exists simply because the Feds wouldn't allow 7mm-'06 and 6.5mm-'06 rifles. Winchester standardized the .30-'06 case necked down to .277" as the .270 Winchester in 1925. I don't know why the Feds allowed it, because it was intended to provide the same performance as the 7mm-'06 and 6.5mm-'06. But to correctly duplicate the efficiency and the versatility of the 7mm-'06 and 6.5mm-'06, the bullet diameter should have been .274"; to split the difference between the .264" 6.5mm and the .284" 7mm. The bullet weights for big game hunting should have been 130 grains, 150 grains, and 170 grains. The rifling twist should have been selected by applying the Greenhill formula to a 170 grain spitzer boattail. That would probably have produced a twist of one turn in 8" or one turn in 8.5". Instead the .270 had a bullet diameter of .277" and a rifling twist of one turn in 10". The slow twist was forced upon Winchester by the Feds. But Winchester loaded the ammunition to very high chamber pressures which gave the 130 grain bullet a muzzle velocity of approximately 3140 fps. That gave the bullet a rotational velocity which would produce an explosive effect. Between 1925 and 1948 the .270 Winchester was the only factory loaded high velocity cartridge which would zap a big game animal dead in its tracks with a lung shot using a bullet of sectional density adequate for big game hunting. Sometime around 1975 the Feds started messing with the .270 Winchester. They said that the high chamber pressures would eventually cause excessive headspace, which could blow up the rifle. The factory ammunition was loaded to lower pressures which produced lower velocities, so it wouldn't zap 'em dead any more. The Feds could have dealt with handloaders who continued to use high velocity loads by slipping them cartridges designed to blow up their rifles. So everybody switched to the 7mm Remington Magnum. The .270 could have zapped 'em dead at safe chamber pressure levels if it had been standardized with a faster rifling twist. But it would have been better to have had 7mm-'06 and 6.5mm-'06 rifles with the proper twist and good bullets.

The other good thing you can do with a .30-'06 case is neck it up to fire .358 caliber bullets. The long, heavy bullets originally used in small bore cartridges gave good penetration but poor killing power. Increasing the bullet diameter with the same type of bullet allows you to keep the penetration and increase the killing power too. In 1922 James Howe invented a .35 caliber wildcat on the .30-'06 case and called it the .35 Whelen. The Feds wouldn't allow that as a standardized cartridge until the late 1980's or the early 1990's. The very similar 9.3X62mm European cartridge dates back to 1905. The .350 Remington Magnum was invented because the Feds wouldn't allow a .35 Whelen, but the Feds forced it to be standardized with too slow a twist to stabilize a 285 or 300 grain bullet; one turn in 16" instead of 12". The 6.5mm Remington Magnum was invented because the Feds wouldn't allow a 6.5mm-'06, but it had too slow a twist; one turn in 9" instead of 7.5".

I'll quit trying to explain every detail about every cartridge and summarize the main points. Although there are a few exceptions, generally;

The Feds have been opposed to fast rifling twists all of the twentieth century, because that's what zaps 'em dead and stabilizes a heavy bullet. Whenever a new cartridge is introduced which is capable of either high velocity for zapping 'em dead, or of firing a heavy bullet of high sectional density for deep penetration on dangerous game, the Feds try to force the manufacturers to standardize with too slow a twist. Examples of too slow a twist include the .350 Remington Magnum, the .280 Remington, the .270 Winchester, the 6.5mm Remington Magnum, all of the .25 caliber cartridges, the .244 Remington, the .243 Winchester, and most of the .22 caliber rifles, notably the M16A1. Any caliber smaller than .30 caliber should have a rifling twist faster than one turn in 10", but most people haven't realized that until recently. The Feds have known it all along, and have been forcing the use of the one in 10" twist with the deliberate intention of reducing the efficiency, killing power, and versatility of small bore cartridges. The reason they didn't force the use of the one in 10" twist with 7mm and 6.5mm rifles is that it was known that a faster twist was required to stabilize their heaviest bullets. But they tried to force too slow a twist on the 7mm Remington Magnum and failed because it was too soon after the fiasco with the .244 Remington.

Whenever a new cartridge is standardized which is capable of firing a medium weight bullet at a velocity which will zap 'em dead, sooner or later the Feds will mess with that bullet. But with premium bullets made by a Fed manufacturer, instead of making a no-good bullet they stop manufacturing that specific bullet weight. The heavier bullets which won't zap 'em dead aren't messed with.

The Feds won't allow bolt action rifles to be made with the safety located in the right place to be operated quickly and easily. There are some exceptions, though. Some bolt action rifles have been made with the safety located on the tang, shotgun style. Exceptions include the Browning A-Bolt, the Savage 110, the original version of the Ruger 77, some Swedish rifles, and some German rifles. But most bolt action rifles have the safety located at the side of the rear of the receiver on the same side as the bolt handle. Any left-handed shooter can tell you that that safety is in the right place for a left-handed shooter. It is in the wrong place for a right-handed shooter. A safety located at the side of the rear of the receiver should be on the side opposite from the bolt handle. Then it would be convenient to operate with the thumb. Putting it on the same side as the bolt handle forces the shooter to have to move his thumb around to the wrong side of the rifle to operate it. That is very awkward and anyone with a lick of sense knows it's wrong. So why didn't the manufacturers fix it 50 or 75 years ago? Because the Feds wouldn't allow it; they wanted that safety to be awkward to operate.

The Feds don't want left-handed people to have good left-handed bolt action rifles. So far as I know, there wasn't any such thing as a left-handed bolt action rifle before World War II, just conversions. After World War II different manufacturers started making them. The Feds would leave them alone for a while, and then start messing with them, so another manufacturer would start making them. Almost all of the bolt action rifle manufacturers have made left-handed rifles, but at any given time just a couple of them were made right, normally Weatherby and one of the others. The others were no-good. The code for a good left-handed bolt action rifle used to be the right, or a photo showing it on the right side of some other rifles. But they may have changed that since I've written about it. For non-conspirators it used to be safer to use a converted rifle, but it might not be these days.

19. <u>U.S. military equipment.</u> In 1990 the U.S. military was still using a gas mask that dated back to the Korean War. That gas mask has filters located inside the mask. To change filters you must remove the mask. But since the Korean War persistent nerve gases have been developed which remain lethal for longer than the filters remain effective. That would kill anyone wearing those masks. Other nations use gas masks which have the filters located externally, so the filters can be changed without removing the mask. The only possible motive for refusing to adopt an improved gas mask is treason.

When lasers were first invented in the 1950's the Feds saw the military potential immediately and began planning ahead. The Feds knew that Star Wars lasers in geosynchronous orbit could rule the world, because they could zap anything below them, on the surface of the planet or in the atmosphere. So the Feds intended to make sure that Russia had Star Wars lasers and the United States didn't, and that the United States was armed with missiles which could be shot down by the lasers. Beginning in the 1950's the Feds deliberately encouraged the use of missiles as anti-aircraft and anti-tank weapons by the U.S. military. Most of the anti-aircraft missiles were in fact more effective than existing anti-aircraft gun weapon systems. Anti-aircraft missiles were necessary until the development of electromagnetic propulsion rail guns. But the anti-tank missile which the Feds mandated for the U.S. military in the 1960's was not in any way an improvement over existing anti-tank weapon systems. It's called the TOW missile, and there are a whole bunch of things wrong with it.

It replaced the recoilless rifle, which was a man-portable weapon. But the TOW missile launcher is too heavy and cumbersome to be man-portable. TOW missile launchers which were intended to be hand-held inflicted injuries on soldiers who attempted to fire missiles from them. The launchers ended up being mounted on motor vehicles. That makes it practically impossible to fire them from a concealed position or a prepared defensive position which would give some protection to the gunner. The missile isn't fire-and-forget; it must be guided to the target. The gunner must continue aiming at the target until the missile hits it. If the gunner is hit the missile will miss. The missile travels very slowly, proceeding by spurts from its rocket. It takes approximately 15 seconds for it to travel 1000 yards. That's an eternity in combat, and the gunner is vulnerable the entire time. Enemy gunners can see where the missile came from and fire at the launcher and gunner. The missile flies downrange trailing a wire behind it which carries the guidance commands. If something cuts the wire the missile will miss. And the missile itself can be shot down by small arms fire because it is so slow.

During the 1970's the Russians made a break-through in laser power output. They immediately applied it to ordinary red lasers. The increased output makes the red lasers powerful enough to blind many types of electronic imaging systems and the human eye. In 1973 the Russians used a red laser with the increased power output to blind a U.S. early warning satellite. The Feds lied and said that the satellite was blinded by the light of a fire. During the 1980's the Russians applied the increased power output to larger Star Wars lasers which produce a beam that is invisible to the human eye and equipped their tanks with red lasers to blind enemy anti-tank gunners.

If there were war between the U.S. and Russia, TOW missiles would be completely ineffective at stopping Russian tanks. Some of the gunners would be blinded by red lasers. Some of the gunners would be hit by enemy fire. Some of the guidance wires would be cut. Most of the TOW missiles which didn't miss for any other reason would be shot down by space-based lasers. Anything you use against tanks where the tanks can shoot back has to be high speed fire-and-forget, and it shouldn't be missiles because lasers can shoot down the missiles. I expect electromagnetic propulsion rail guns to be used as both anti-aircraft and anti-tank guns during World War III. High value targets will be defended by lasers, of course.

U. S. Navy torpedoes were made to be ineffective against Russian submarines. The Mark 46 had a 100 pound warhead which would not sink a double-hulled Russian submarine unless it hit near the propeller shaft. It probably wouldn't sink the titanium-hulled submarines at all. The Mark 48 had a larger warhead but only a 5 knot speed advantage over a Russian sub. If the sub detected the torpedo from a distance of a few thousand yards the sub could out-run the torpedo. It was possible to build a faster torpedo because the British did it. But the Feds didn't want us to have torpedoes which would be effective against Russian submarines.

The M1 Abrams tank has a main gun and armor which are inferior to those of a Russian tank. The main gun of the Abrams must be manually reloaded each shot; it is the equivalent of an 1870's single shot rifle. The main gun of a Russian tank reloads automatically; it is the equivalent of a 1930's Garand semiautomatic rifle. The Russian tank can deliver a higher rate of fire, which almost always gives tactical superiority. The ceramic armor in the Abrams' turret is made of flat slabs which are cast separately and then inserted into cavities in the turret. That leaves gaps between the slabs. The ceramic armor of a Russian tank is cast in the turret itself. That gives a solid layer of ceramic without any gaps. If U.S. tanks and Russian tanks fight without U.S. airpower entering into the battle, the Russian tanks will win every time. And the Russians have lasers with which to destroy U.S. airpower. The United States could build tanks with armor and firepower equal to Russian tanks, but the Feds don't want us to.

Apache helicopters and Aegis cruisers are both made wrong too, but I don't feel like explaining exactly what's wrong with them. It doesn't matter anyway because in a war with Russia they would both be destroyed by Russian lasers. It wouldn't do any good to fix what's wrong with them.

I have been out of touch for several years. Some of the deficiencies I've described may have been corrected by now. They may have adopted a better gas mask, our torpedoes might have larger warheads, and the main gun of an Abrams might reload automatically. But for many years these things were true, and they show a pattern of treason from within the Federal government.

During the Vietnam War the Feds put an additive into gunpowder used to load ammunition for the M16 rifle. That rifle has a gas tube which pipes gas from the barrel back to the receiver. Gas from the tube pushes the bolt carrier back to eject the fired case and chamber another cartridge automatically. The Feds found an additive called calcium carbonate which would clog up the gas tube of the rifle. The M16 got a bad reputation for jamming, but it wasn't anything wrong with the rifle; it was poisoned gunpowder. It is quite likely that the Feds wouldn't have allowed the M16 to be adopted unless they knew from the first how to mess with it. The excuse for putting calcium carbonate into the gunpowder was to stabilize the powder, but other stabilizers work just as well, so they don't put calcium carbonate into gunpowder any more. Poisoning the gunpowder was an act of treason during wartime. My source for this is the March 1984 issue of American Rifleman magazine, page 34. The magazine article doesn't say that it was done deliberately. I'm telling you that the Federation conspiracy does things like that deliberately.

There are thousands of consumer products made wrong. If you start looking you will find some I haven't mentioned. With most types of consumer products, if you buy the wrong brand you get something that is poisonous or no-good, but another brand is okay. What type of consumer product did you stop using? Can you understand why you switched to a different product?

Part C: Stuff the Feds Don't Allow

1. <u>Blankets.</u> From the 1960's to the 1990's the Feds didn't allow inexpensive blankets made of synthetic fiber. You could buy a comforter or an electric blanket or an expensive wool Hudson's Bay blanket, but you couldn't buy a regular blanket. For many years there weren't any for sale in the stores. Then in 2001 while one of my relatives was working at a fabric shop, she sent me a scarf made of fleece fabric as a Christmas present. I asked her if that fabric was available in sizes suitable for a blanket. She sent me a small sheet of it. That's why the Feds allowed fleece blankets. But just like the one my relative gave me, they aren't quite big enough to cover the bed, so you have to buy a pair of them and sew them together. My best guess as to why the Feds wouldn't allow regular blankets is that they want poor homeless people to die of the cold. Wealthy people can heat their house.

2. Hydrogen powered automobiles.

3. Men's wallets made of vinyl instead of leather.

4. Aluminum sailboats.

5. Ferrocement boats, sail or power.

6. 6.5mm-'06 rifles with a rifling twist of one turn in 7.5".

7. Missile defenses and bomb shelters and stuff for bomb shelters.

8. Sevin insecticide.

9. Aluminum garbage cans, and lots of other things which should be made of aluminum because they rust.

10. Safety devices to prevent airplane crashes.

11. Hollofill insulated parkas with Hollofill insulated hoods.

12. Improved typewriter keyboards to allow faster typing.

CHAPTER 9
CODE

The code I can give you is obsolete even before this is published. The conspiracies know I'm writing this, and they know how much code I know, so they are changing their languages and usage. The information I give should be used to try to translate commercials, TV shows, and songs that were written before 1995.

There are many different code languages. Until I started writing this, each conspiracy had a language for open messages to its own conspirators. Open messages don't need to be kept secret from enemy conspirators, just from hypnotized people. For messages they need to keep secret from enemies they use other languages. Conspiracies are constantly inventing new code words and new code languages to replace code that has been broken by the enemy. Once a code word has been broken by the enemy, it can be used for open messages. The result is that there are many different code words for the things that are talked about most often. I haven't attempted to learn any of the code used for secret messages. The code used for open messages is difficult enough for me. I haven't learned very much of it. A child who has been a conspirator for just a few years knows more code than I have learned in twenty years. But I have learned enough of it to prove that it exists to someone who is willing to make an effort to verify it.

Code is easiest to spot in short forms; jokes, advertising slogans, proverbs, nursery rhymes, poems, and songs. Code in a full length novel is more difficult to spot. Nursery rhymes are devices for teaching code to children. I don't know how else they teach code or I would have learned more of it. Words used as titles are code. Often the story will explain the translation. Code can sound like nonsense to an innocent person. If someone who should know better says something that isn't true or doesn't make sense, it's probably code.

The quickest and easiest way to spot code words is to look for modifier words. The modifier tells which language to translate that word in. The conspirators know each other's languages used for open messages, so they often borrow words from other conspiracies' languages. The modifier might be either in front of or after the word it modifies. Most of the modifiers are listed as conspiracy names, because they use conspiracy names to indicate which conspiracy's language should be used to translate the word which is being modified. Fed name means translate as Fed code, and so forth.

Spotting a code word isn't the same thing as translating it. To translate it you either have to have a pretty good idea of what they are talking about, or see it used often enough to assign a translation based on context. Then you have to test the translation to see if it makes sense each time. Make certain that you are testing it in the correct language. You might not be able to verify the translation of a Fed code word if you test it against something written by Mafia or Nazis.

Just reading the code I've listed isn't going to prove it to anyone. To verify it you have to apply it, and to apply it you either have to memorize it or computerize it. You should use a computer to keep track of translations, code words you have spotted but can't translate, and words that might be code.

Ideally you should be able to type in a passage and have the computer mark and translate the code words. When using text printed on paper I mark code words by drawing boxes around them and write the translations above. I use dotted boxes for words that might be code and I put a question mark where I don't know or am not certain of the translation. I use a curved arrow from the modifier pointing to the word it modifies, and use a straight arrow if it modifies a phrase or group of words. You'll need to program your computer to mark the words in a similar fashion. It would be helpful for the computer to translate a passage first in one language and then in another to see which language makes sense.

For this version, when I give a usage example I'll mark the code words with an outline type font. But I'm not going to give very many usage examples. I was forced to delete most of my usage examples and sneakers because they were song lyrics. Copyright law doesn't allow me to use them without permission. I will include a few that are in the public domain.

The most basic code word is love, from Mafia code. They hypnotize someone with pleasure and say that he did it for love. Whenever they use a hypnotized person against their enemies, or by extension carry out any operation or attack against another conspiracy they call it love. The Mafia also says they love something if they are against it because it is bad or no-good. The Nazis say they love something if they like it and want good things for it, and sometimes use love to mean sex. But usually the word love by itself means an attack by a conspiracy; something they can do to destroy their enemies and increase their own power. Feds might say romance instead of love, and use "on the balcony" to mean "in love."

Nazi alphabet

A = bad for you, good for them.   Nazi hypnosis--
B = ? sting?   ER, BER, DER,
C = ? seeing is believing?   HER, KER, SER,
D = done? dead?
E = ? (Different from the Mafia E.) ERA = ? EPA = ?
F = ?   ESP = ? EST = ?
G = ?
H = ?
I = our I see K is?
J = ?
K = stick = threat
L = ?
M = ?
N = ?
O = ?

P = ?

Q = ?

R = our

S = mean ? = cruelty

T = ?

U = Mafia

V = ?

W = ?

X = ?

Y = around = vulnerable

Z = blame or drum = provide sex hypnosis

Names for Nazi, modifiers to indicate Nazi usage.
D, 6, K, BA, BC, Bo, MC, Mac, SS, ZZ, wolf, shark, condor, vulture, buzzard, crocodile, alligator, cannibals, nobody, brick, nation, the nation, national, country, the country, hell, shell, shade, devil, the devil, Satan, satin, Atlantis, raisin, grapevine, delta, triangle, new, new age, third age, Third Reich, countrymen, no fear, no worries, no sweat, Richard, Bubba, Jack, Rick, Nick, Gordon, Ryan, Roy, Wallace?, Jerry, ARC, Flintstones, Kzinti, Indiana, Egyptian, Viking, Cheyenne, Spanish Inquisition, Baker?, coyote, Chevy?, Islam, Phoenix, thunderbird, thunderbolt, two lightning bolts, the warriors, medicine man (= poisons Feds), witch doctor (= murders whores), warrior, free men, Fremen (Dune), believe it or not, ECO, echo, the economy, means, the county?, attitude, tree hugger, rising sun, chicken rancher?, rat, rats, inquiring mind, brute?, boy, the boy, boys, the boys, force, the force, beetle, true, the truth, power, the power, cause, the cause, beast, the beast, bear, the bear, PAK, pack, the pack, the village, hamer, hammer,

quail?, brother, airborne, sunflowers, goat roper?, rhythm, serious?, foreman?, interest?, (The Mafia says that some of those are wrong, but I don't know which ones.)

Nazi salute-- arm extended up and/or forward, or raised fist.

Nazi hypnosis-- discipline, drive them to it, push a button, mean, number, beat, motivation, interesting?, crater?, harass?, cringe?, bother, rattle, hassle, share?, tick?, hire?, force, begin, raise, crank, break, sweat, care, core, cane, cage, bug, haze, box?, raised by wolves,

Sex hypnosis by Nazis-- go, room (for murder), big, hope, KIM, time, John, Johnny, Paul, Gomer, Rambo, Jimbo, bimbo, Bojangles, MEG?, retro?, London?, hamer, hammer, rush?,

Mafia alphabet--

A = male sex organ

B = breasts, by extension; pornography.

C = sea = see

D = Nazis

E = enters

F = fight, or fix = kill

G = job   Mafia hypnosis- AM, MA, IM,

H = ?   OP, POP, OB, OO, ON, SON,

I = eye = provide sex hypnosis   OR, NN, OJ, JO, LO,

J = hook or angle = hypnosis

K = maleness

L = like = prefer

M = murder

N = in

O = oh! or come = sex hypnosis

P = I love you = death and destruction to you.

Q = sexual turn-on
R = our
S = is
T = ? porn?
U = ?
V = down = bad
W = double you = poison (Rev. Ch. 18.)
X = Feds, and unknown = the Feds poisoned it or messed with it; destroyed it.
Y = femaleness
Z = ?

Names for Mafia, modifiers to indicate Mafia usage--

Eve, even, seven, 7, ever, every, everybody, jet, jets, us, US, United States, U, you, your, we're your.....(fill in the blank), J, whore, the whore, Air Force, so, Dixie, GI, CB?, special forces, minute man, missionaries, Christian?, friends, the environment, the struggle?, violence, population, universal, horizon?, challenge, challenger, long, longer, person, gator, square?, France, Japan, Japanese, Oklahoma?, Seminoles?, Cherokees?, soon?, Cordell, Mudville, Martians (The War of The Worlds), girl, the girl, girls, the girls, Alice, Ann, Annie, Diana, Dorothy, Jill, Lucy, Lucille, Mary, Cooper?, Conner, Dick, Edward?, Howard?, Simmons?, colonist, the colonists, old, mason?, angler, catcher, the catcher, mother, energy, Toyota?, Bugs Bunny, sisters, city, evil, queen, widow, witch, grant, glory, order, camp, high, wood, woods, would, mob?, the mob?, I, eye, now, oh, honey?, uncle, American (X),

Mafia salute-- Hand to the head.

Mafia hypnosis-- fascinating, slip into shock, the

same, order, gone, name, rogers?, moon?

Hypnotized by Mafia-- intellectual, best friend, observer, Casey, victim?, customer?, actor?, sport?, blind, twin, twins, baby, pet, frog, dog, cop, Sam,

Nazi hypnosis by Mafia-- Sherwood?, Destry?, sweaters?, diner?, hulk?,

Fed alphabet--

A = kill or destroy OR = poison ON = poison

B = ?   AL = destroy pleasure

C = ?

D = ?

E = ?

F = ?

G = ?

H = ?

I = ? Mafia?

J = ?

K = Nazis

L = ? pleasure?

M = ?

N = ?

O = circle or ring or arch = poison

P = ?

Q = ?

R = ?

S = ? means?

T = cruise = crucify (Not literally; figuratively!)

U = ?

V = ?

W = ?

X = truce ? ceasefire? stop it?

Y = ?

Z = 30 or the end = death

Names for Fed, modifiers to indicate Fed usage--
magician, X, 9, OZ, UN, AB, DU, AK, OK?, SA,
SAS?, UP, UPS, PAR, ARM, Army, the army,
Abe?, Abraham?, sun, Sunday, sunshine, rain,
reign, king, the king, the kings, the kingdom, the
king of ..... (fill in the blank), law, the law, state, the
state, crew, the crew, Roman, the Romans, coach,
the coach, man, the man, men, the men, God, rey,
real, royal, town, civic?, some, somebody, some
kind of .... (fill in the blank), authority, the authorities, fed, federal, federation, the federation, the en-
terprise, company, the company, CIA, bureau, the
bureau, bureaucrat, excellence, concentration, The
Shadow, will, William, George, Adam, Adams,
Murphy, Tom, Mark (U), O'Conner, McArthur,
McDonald, MacLean, Columbia, America (U), So-
viets, Sioux?, Choctaw?, Elmer Fudd, checkist,
dicta, wizard, citizen, all, all of us, ways, always,
lighthouse, master, puppeteer, Pierson's puppeteer,
standard, spiral, abba, father, dad, daddy, sickle,
scythe, total, monitor, central, warden, union,
united, science, monopoly, mother nature, intelligence, the Colonel, Raiders?, inevitable?, chroni-
cle?, lodge?, weather,
Fed salute-- Arm across chest.
Feds allied with Nazis-- ways and means, news
and weather, arm and hammer, hammer and sickle,
Coordinated Universal Time, heat and humidity,
Feds allied with Mafia-- Adam and Eve, law and
order, Greenwich Mean Time,
Fed hypnosis-- borg, light, chain, acted?, directed?,
check?, crystal?, controlled?,
Hypnotized by Feds-- client, machine, robot, pup-

pet, cartoon, toon, tune, Arthur, agent, shadow, dummy, the Senator?,

Sex hypnosis by Feds-- max, marx, janine, robin, magnum, loreal, J.R.?, Russell?, Rio?, jungle?, chambers?, junior?,

Nazi hypnosis by Feds-- border, the border, hat?, Herman?, Sherman?, box?, boxer?,

Conspiracy names and modifiers I can't translate-- brick wall, road, the road, digital, GM, GAR, puppet masters, MIT, dammit, Hatfields, McCoys, champion, hunter, decent, firm, civilization, REM, the Saint, common, modern, progressive, Henderson, Texas, Kramer, Cramer, bean, ranger, duke, Gibson, you can trust ..... (fill in the blank), Smith, Jones, braves, volunteers, foundation, empire, TEK, tech, technology, tide, IRA, Irish, Kelly, Troy, Hogan, Krueger, Simpson, Christopher, YO, York, Simon, Campbell, POLY, scorpion, people, the people, mud people, diversity, society, farmer, network, domino, pepper, rainbow, family, I am, horns, the public, rain forest, well, wells, mighty, control, Kaos, chaos, this, care bears, emerge, emerging, tiger, the eagle, the lion, Reds, the Reds, star, the stars, JA, Mister, Mr. Wilson, Mr. Rogers, GE, Ford, AIM, ET, Jetsons, boss, the boss, dictator, ordinary,

Code-- mathematics (X), business (U), transmission, language, traffic, speech, slang, mail,

Code that isn't code-- business trip, password, key word,

Next word isn't code-- generally? (X), ain't, little (U), probably, just, very, **Nulls**-- (Most nulls are also modifiers to indicate that the next word isn't code.) never (X&D?), if (D), but (X), can't, don't, no, almost (U),

Kill or destroy-- hit, punch, make a decision, drive, tell, save, focus, engage, express (X), rite, ritual, sacrifice, rap, ram, ramp, step on, trip, there, serve, eat, protect, knot, not, survive (D), touch, reach out and touch, fight, fix, met, laugh, bring flowers to (U), call (U&D?), know (D&X) = gets killed or destroyed, life (U&X) = what kills or destroys you.

Declaration of intent to kill or destroy-- want, wanted, measure (X), hungry, looks good to me? (D), I'm sorry, promise, promises (U), searching for, send you to school, teach you a lesson (U&D),

Die, or dead, or death-- alive, future (X), peace?, destiny, destination, the other side, happy, here, heaven (D), late, cry (U), the beach, forever, nothing, fall down, fine, famous, China (?)

Hit man-- thief, plumber, mechanic, safe cracker, safe driver, doctor, judge, sheriff, executive, Sherlock Holmes, gardener, carpenter, soldier, fighter, cook, Eddie, Freddie, Michael, ferret?,

Woman you have sex with while hypnotized- deputy, Dr. Watson, maid, nanny, nurse, secretary, sister,

Hypnosis-- trance, transport, spell, freeze, frozen, enchantment, 10, acted, directed, another world, losing consciousness,

Jail or prison-- refrigerator, restaurant, hospital, airport, factory, school, toilet,

You get arrested-- school, college, sheepskin, minute, New York minute, professional, tow truck, alley, RR, lawyer, shower, rapids, rest, ant, married, wedding, bride, I do, say I do, Indian, kid, child, children, anything, anybody, Australia, wiseguy, corner, collar, lake, landing, money, pig, day, time, Rocky, Rockies, taxi to the airport, taxi driver, ambulance to the hospital, ambulance driver, MY, my life, 18, west,

Information they feed you-- line, wire, sign, pill,

What you're hooked on -- air, crutch, monkey, drug. Drug = something you're hooked on that is poisoned, or will be. D.R.U.G = Nazi our Mafia job.

While under hypnosis-- basement (U?), downstairs? (X), north (?), underground (D?), lights off (U), black person (U&D?), left hand, left foot, drunk, wearing sunglasses,

While conscious-- attic (U?), upstairs? (X), south (?), aboveground (D?), lights on (U), white person (U), in your right mind, right hand, right foot, **Lies to fool you**-- story, load, bull, hay (D), cloud, fog (X), nightmare, snow, cotton (U), sand, dust, smoke, garbage, light, static (?) Forest = false belief.

Sex hypnosis operation-- jungle, whorehouse, lever, bar, steam room, club,

Television-- radar, microwave, music box, satellite, satellite radio, mirror, billboard,

Scared, or scared into running away-- parachute, chicken, cream, reflex,

What scares you-- thunder, spider, bear, lion, button, heavy,

Run away-- motorcycle, fly, learn to fly (D&X?), duck (X), run, beat it?, roll? (U), go home (U&D), breakout, get out of town, go fishing, blow, skip, bolt?, leap, jump (from the bridge, or plane, or tall building), Geronimo (?) **Smoking**-- back (U), nun, rabbit, carrot (U&D), leaf, leaves (X), but, butt (D), weed? (D)

Figure out code, or whatever-- sneak, follow, chase, catch, get, make, take, gather, handle, scan, read, trace, copy,

Dangerous-- bad, easy, a piece of cake, graceful?

Sex-- dance (D&X?), coffee (U), football, poker, poke, canoeing, key, picking pockets, wrestling,

Breasts-- bees, tomatoes, cones, martini,

Porn-- bait (D), art, drink, cheers, lace, wine, oil, steam, LA (porn men like; U), AL (porn women like; U),

It frames you-- shoot, kill, die, dirt, turn, blood, walk, herd, chip? (D), pain, paint, pattern, emotion, emotional content (X), piece, wind, wings, swing, hang, change, pump, stamp, trap,

Porn to frame you-- leg, place, part, pair?, mile, taxes, lash, slash, quarter, pebbles, bubbles, champagne, golden BB, killer bees, killer tomatoes, rope, heroin, whipped cream, hair, combing your hair in the mirror, hang glider, silence, tick?,

Porn to help you-- whip it, OPP (D)

Porn to send messages-- lips, read my lips, come & get it, beer (B ear), rear view mirror, you can't take it with you when you go, traffic cones, air traffic, airmail,

It means not, or the opposite-- a stutter (U?), and at the beginning of the sentence, as....(fill in the blank)...as (D), got to, gotta, still (X), at least, already, something repeated three times in a song,

What you believe-- buy, bicycle (buy cycle), binoculars (buy noculars), swallow, ride, horse, bell, ring a bell,

You're wrong-- sure, I am not so sure, I think, no doubt, says, incredible?

Being protected by a conspiracy-- clothes, watch, safe, home, pool, swimming pool, covered, bank. Usage example for the word watch: Famous phrase from a book which translates as Nazi sex hypnosis is protecting the Mafia.

Person being protected-- hero, star?

Numbers-- 0 = sex hypnosis when pronounced oh, 0 = poison when pronounced zero. 1 = male sex organ (U). 1 = dead or destroyed (X). 2 = poison (U). 2 = to (X?). 3 = a lie or something false. 4 = for (D). 5 = F.I.V.E. = kill eye bad enters = if they can portray it as a threat, then they can do it to you. 6 = fear, or Nazis. 7 = S Eve N, or Mafia. 8 = ate = killed or poisoned (D). 9 = Feds. 10 = hypnotized. 11 = ? 12 = ? 13 = murder. 14 = ? 15 = wrong answer, mistake, false belief. 16 = sweet = ? 17 = ? 18 = you get arrested. 19 = immediately? Something bad the Feds do? 20 = ? 30 = death from something, or the end of something. 40 = For T Y = you get crucified. (Figuratively.) 46 = crucified with Nazi hypnosis. 47 = crucified with Mafia hypnosis. 50 = not any more. 60 = ? 70 = ? 80 = ? 90 = The Feds get you or kill you? 95 = The Feds' big lie technique. Tell a lie and make it come true. Say that it causes cancer and then poison it with carcinogenic additives. 100 = ? 1,000 = sand = a lie to fool you, or false belief. 1,000,000 = lethal, death, dying.

Number Usage Examples-- 911 = Fed destruction destroyed. 90210 = Fed sex hypnosis to destroy sex hypnosis. 1040 = hypnosis for crucifixion. AK 47 = Feds crucifying with Mafia hypnosis.

Colors-- red = fire = trouble. green = go. yellow = afraid. blue = ? gray = dead? (D). black = secret or hypnotized (U). white = not secret or conscious (U). white = poison (D). gold = everything. brown = provide sex hypnosis (U&X?).

City nicknames-- City names are usually code themselves, but nicknames give other code meanings for different conspiracies. Most of these are Fed nicknames given in Mafia or Nazi code, but the first one is in Fed code. Athens = first in honor (X). Baltimore = monumental (U). Boston = hub (U). Calcutta = black hole. Dallas = big (D). Denver = mile high (U). Detroit = motor (U). Miami = magic (U). Tokyo = heart of Japan.

Poison, or poisoned, or made wrong-- (These aren't sorted by conspiracy.) arrow (X), honor? (X), bullet (X), shoot (X), medicine (X), only (X), only one (U or X?), natural, only natural, concentrated (X), favorite (U), drug, more (X), diamonds, diamond ring, metric?, small, skillet, point (D), Smokey (cigarettes), something, high school, highway, way, halfway, long way, come a long way, rain, wet, humidity, gone (D), 2, 2 percent, 2 million, 95, 95 percent, 95 seconds, seconds, in seconds, hydrated? (D), dehydrated?, genetic (X), grass, lawnmower, sickle, scythe, lunch, double, ton, tun, cycles, pass the ......(U&D), toxic waste, intoxicated, little (X), MM, FF, quant. suff., enough, time enough, stripes, zebra, circle, ring, arch, golden ring, golden arch, crop circles, Cali, California, secret, the secret is in ....(fill in the blank), secret recipe, rich man's recipe, fire extinguisher, man on the moon, smooth, close encounter, great taste, tastes great, it tastes like chicken, hole, whole, corn, popcorn, lean, lean on, getaway, air pollution, field, Polish, pure, cure, alien, loaded (U), meteor, meteorite, ox, pox, oxy, oxidant, rust (X), melt, the other, medium, seed (D), junk food, junk.... (fill in the blank), bacteria (War of The Worlds), germs, worm, worms, close-up, rich, miracle, ugly?, fair, fair dinkum, steel, steal, delicious (D), good for you (X), what I need (X), too much (U), better, water (D), hill (D), pail (D), pale (D), mine (sort of, sometimes; X), no ..... (fill in the blank) (D), four (U). The Feds use code for poison falsely to scare off enemy conspirators, and their code which tells whether it is really poisoned is secret code. New products are often given a name which means it is poisoned while they wait to see if the Feds will poison it.

Antidote-- antioxidant

Poisoned person-- not afraid any more (U), hillbilly (D), grasshopper (D), satisfied customer, zombie (the living dead), miner (X), graduate, guilty?, millionaire, rich man, smart, genius, Einstein, oxymoron, wetback, winner, sergeant, Chinese person,

Not poisonous, or made right-- premium, the right....(fill in the blank), your choice?, most popular? But you might as well disregard those, because the Feds have probably started poisoning everything with those labels. The safest way to tell whether something is poisoned is to see if a conspirator will eat it. But be careful, because some things might require an antidote, and some things that aren't poisonous by themselves are poisonous in combination with something else.

False poisons-- less, less filling, stainless steel?, rhinestone?, natural light, close encounter of the third kind, 6 carat diamond, 222, WWW, sandwich, circles in the sand, worm riding, faking an orgasm, falsely believing that you ate the whole thing. Usually the Feds poison just what the doctor ordered, but they started using false poisons on everything all at once in 1986 in the United States. The false poisons cause pain, to hurt you and make you think that you are getting cancer. That makes you quit smoking or drinking or whatever the Mafia has you hypnotized with. That is one of the fulfillments of Rev. Ch. 18 vs. 4. Another is that Jews from the United States began immigrating to Israel in large numbers in 1990 or 1991. What I've written might be another.

Other words-- party = war (U). Mars = war (X). greenhouse, septic tank = bomb shelter. pterodactyl = ICBM (dinosaur bird = extinction flies.) Napoleon factory = insane asylum. over = done or finished. under = done or finished. ahead of = they know what you will do; they are prepared. truck & bus = what they hit you with? train = travel with protection from a conspiracy to a pre-planned destination. ship = ? boat = what keeps you afloat? submarine = conspiracy. airplane = L.E.G. = plan enters with the air. gyrocopter = hero copter. bridge = be ours I. D. job enters. My bridges were movies on TV. Watch the movie, jump, and they pick you up. Jump from the bridge into the river. (Sneaker for river; song lyrics I cannot use.) house = country or nation (U?). bedroom = where the baby is. kitchen = ? the world = the Feds and their allies of

the moment, usually the Nazis. hand = what someone does. head is sometimes what you believe, but
sometimes what you are hooked on. conehead =
breast fixated. butthead = cigarette fixated. canoe-
head = sex fixated. Pictures of people with something above and behind their head are code. helmet
= keeps ideas from penetrating. cap with earflaps =
keeps you from hearing what the other conspiracy is
saying. knife is similar to five; threat in eye kill enters. pistol has something to do with seeing porn,
maybe porn they are feeding you to help you. rifle; I
don't know, but it defeats a pistol. shotgun = truth
that can be used against someone. sawed-off shotgun = your truth isn't going to prove it. milk coun-
teracts blood. young usually means weak or strong,
sometimes usually means this time or not this time,
but different conspiracies use them differently. heart
= power (U&X). spit = rejection. sneaker & poetry
= code breaking; translating code. mountain = death
and destruction (U&D). grandmother and grandfa-
ther = mother & father (U&D). Two different uses
for the word not occur with the form something, not
something else. With the first use, both somethings
are code and the not is either a null or it means and.
With the second use, either of the somethings might
or might not be code, and the not means kill or destroy, but the second something destroys the first.
I've seen not used as kill or destroy at the beginning
of the sentence in a book written by a Fed author.
I've seen not used as a null, but I don't know which
conspiracy's language it is.

In some books and movies some of the events
occur in reverse sequence. A book might have a se-

ries of events planned for the protagonist, in code, in reverse, and another series of events about what another conspiracy will be doing, in code, in reverse. I know of several different movies for which a correct understanding of the situation requires that a significant event from the ending of the movie be put at the beginning of the movie.

Words with different translations-- walk = They can tell what you are going to do by how you walk (U&D). walk = travel (X). time = sex hypnosis (D). time = you get arrested (U). time = end (X). off = kill or get rid of it (D). off = incorrect (U). shoot = see something that frames you (D). shoot = poison it (X). model = someone who poses (U). model = plan (X). no = no-good (D). no = a null (U). no = false (X). behind = in support of (U). behind = hidden by (D). swim = travel (D). swim = support yourself (U). gone = poisoned (D). gone = hypnotized (U). comet = atomic bomb or nuclear war (U). comet = poison (D?).

Nazi code-- Nazis use phonetic spelling, especially for names. Words which end in S, and might or might not have an apostrophe, are used as code. car = conspiracy. Different types of cars represent the conspiracy doing different things. street = arrested? what = poison? or = because. won't = will. inquiry = torture. draw & walk & turn = you do something they use to frame you. shoot & herd = you see or hear something they use to frame you. war = you think it's a good thing to do but you're wrong. maybe = Mafia defeated or hypnotized. work = Mafia hypnosis? survive = kill. know = gets destroyed. there= the murderer. here = the murder victim. if =

a null. six = fear. voice = messages. white = poison. ton = poison. free = free to die? cross & across = go against. help = ? do something bad to them? load & hay & horse = a lie or false belief. harmonic convergence = getting all of the Nazis to attack the same target? when = now. around = vulnerable. might = should. mountain = death & destruction. of course = yes. before = not any more. through = stopped. some & will & up & always = Fed usage modifiers. now & even & so = Mafia usage modifiers. Can't translate- wilding, move, heat, hate, Texas, ground, depends on, inevitable.

Nazi usage examples--

Mafia hypnosis? makes free to die?

Arbeit macht frei. Work makes free.

The Mafia will be hypnotized vulnerable to death. Now the Mafia gets hypnotized. Mafia will be hypnotized fear

She'll be coming around the mountain when she comes. She'll be driving six

of poison belief. Now the Mafia gets hypnotized

white horses when she comes.

Mafia code-- The Mafia uses lots of nulls. They include can't, don't, almost, no, possibly why, and sometimes never. There are probably some others I haven't spotted. Obeying Mafia orders is to dance or to wait. Wait also means sex hypnosis or provide sex hypnosis. It is derived from a prostitute waiting for a customer. To refuse to obey orders is crazy; they lose their mind. Orders are called music. The conspirators who give orders are called musicians or someone from upstairs. To have a conspiracy working for you is to be lucky. To persuade is to pitch or to sell. salesman = persuader. You can't =

you must. With other forms can't seems to be a null. hurry = stay away from it. speed = intelligence; ability to understand code or figure things out. slow = simple, easy to understand code, or not very smart. miss = fail to notice or understand. stand = stay put and/or withstand. off = wrong. big = important. everyday = hypnotize someone into committing a crime and getting caught. uptown = good for the Mafia, bad for the Nazis and Feds. downtown = bad for the Mafia, good for the Nazis and Feds. swim = to support yourself. drown = unable to support yourself. born = the Nazis get you? imagination = paranoia; ability to anticipate attacks. sleep = ignore events and remain inactive. so & you = Fed usage modifiers. remember = stop using it. carry = keep it going.

Fed code-- The Feds use lots of opposites, such as good means bad & alive means dead & best means worst. They use words with un at the beginning, such as unfortunately meaning fortunate for the Feds and unlimited meaning limited by the Feds. At the end of a sentence, eh? = A = destroy or obstruct that. face = reputation. To save face is to destroy someone's reputation. The word to literally translates as crucifixion poison, but seems to mean destroy the reputation of whatever it refers to. Also literally translates as destroy pleasure with poison, but is used to refer to something secret which cannot be discussed openly. you & so & longer = Mafia usage modifiers. dual & durable & typical & junk = something they messed with. glad = mad. bright = be right? all right = ? the Feds win? come back = they attack or destroy. elapsed time = time until.

may = will. only = poison. if only = next time.
thanks = goodbye. show = demonstration of power
or ability before using it for effect. fire = trouble.
determined = decided. option = something they
have decided to do. forest = false belief. prevent =
cause. more = poison. says = say mistakenly. pain
& paint = public address eye in = mass media to
frame you. never = a null. handle = decode. poison
= keep people from believing something that is true
by falsely creating evidence to the contrary. tres-
passer = non-conspirator who finds out about conspiracies, or about something the Feds want kept
secret. say the magic word = put someone under
hypnosis. closely = wrongly? possibility = cer-
tainty? question = problem (sickle dot). earthquake
= sudden change of circumstances for the worse,
usually but not always seems to mean another conspiracy took control. Can't translate- guarantee,
Destroy?   enslave?

Fed usage examples-- Divide and conquer, unite
and rule. Thumbs up, thumbs down.
Sneakers-- For baseball: It's an old comedy routine
by a comedy duo. For wiseguy: It's a song in an old
movie. For winning: It's one of the famous sayings
of a person associated with sports. For a hand signal: It's a song by an all girl rock band. The British
made a TV show with sneakers for Nazi code.
Hand signals-- Finger alongside the nose = Mafia
recognition signal. It has another meaning that I
don't understand. Turn your head and quickly look
away = too dangerous for contact. Arms crossed in
an X = stop, it's dangerous. Hand on top of head
sliding front to back = too deep for me. Rubbing

thumb and first two fingers together, or opening and closing thumb and first two fingers = that word isn't code. Used most often with the word money, also with crazy and change. Shaking your head "no" while talking = it isn't true. Putting your hand on someone's shoulder for a photograph = I have them hypnotized.

I'm definitely not infallible. Do not give up if you find a mistake. Keep trying and most of it will prove to be correct. Eventually the code will prove to you that conspiracies exist. Don't waste your time trying to tell anyone. Whoever you tell will either be a conspirator who knows about it already but won't admit it, or a hypnotized person who won't believe you. Take it for granted that you are hypnotized by Nazis. The Mafia attempted to use a hypnotized person who knew about conspiracies to destroy the Feds. They failed. The Nazis will try it next. You have a chance to live if you leave the United States quickly enough and the Feds don't find out that you know. You must be certain that you have escaped from your hypnotists before taking the next step. Find someone who is hypnotized; learn the signals that their hypnotists use, prove to them that they are hypnotized, and help them escape from their hypnotists. Start a Christian conspiracy of freed slaves; a conspiracy that doesn't commit acts of death and destruction. God will help you. You are part of His plan.

CHAPTER 10
WHAT REALLY HAPPENED
SEPT. 11ᵀᴴ, 2001

A two hour season premier of a TV show had a story about terrorists crashing a small plane into the White House. Then golfer Payne Stewart and his companions died because their airplane had been rigged by Nazis to depressurize so they would die from lack of oxygen. It was murder made to look like an accident. That dirty trick works on anyone because you cannot tell that you aren't getting enough oxygen; you just faint and then die. The Nazis expected retaliation. An Egyptian airlines pilot planned what he would do if his airliner depressurized. So the Feds hypnotized him into doing it even though the plane wasn't depressurized. He suddenly put the airliner into a steep dive because hypnosis made him think it was depressurized. He was overpowered and the other pilot started to pull the plane out of the dive. At that point the Feds zapped the plane with a Star Wars laser and it crashed. It was theorized that the irrational pilot was an Islamic fanatic, based on the fact that he said a prayer as he dived the plane.

Early in August of 2001 I went to an abstract company to get a copy of a deed. Their executive wouldn't see me immediately so I was forced to wait in the reception room, sitting on their couch with magazines on a table in front of the couch. I picked an aerospace magazine to read while waiting. It had an article about pilotless military aircraft. The Air Force has planes that can take off, fly a combat mission and deliver munitions, return to base and land without a pilot on board and without remote guidance. Computer technology has advanced to the point that an airplane can be flown by a robot pilot in the form of black boxes. My only thought about it at the time was that it was a response to Star Wars lasers. Russian lasers can shoot down any of our planes at any time and the Air Force knows it. So to keep pilots from being killed they develop robot aircraft. A month later I found out how wrong I was. For several days I didn't write down anything about the attacks because I was afraid they were going to come and arrest me. Reading that magazine at the abstract company framed me for getting the idea of how to crash airplanes into buildings. But I didn't. *They* did. The executive at that abstract company is a member of the conspiracy that crashed those airplanes into the World Trade Center and the Pentagon.

Those airplanes were rigged two different ways; they were rigged to depressurize and kill everyone on board, and rigged with black boxes to turn them into guided missiles. It was almost certainly done by U.S. citizens here in the United States. Check the records of those aircraft. When and where was maintenance performed? Where were those planes temporarily grounded that they could have been messed with, not by Islamic terrorists but by Feds?

Everyone on board the planes was dead five or ten minutes after they reached cruising altitude. There weren't any heroes fighting terrorists on the plane that crashed in Pennsylvania. The only evidence of that is from phone calls. The phone calls were faked by electronic technology. The Feds have had technology capable of faking someone's voice on the phone since the early 1980's. A science fiction movie made in the early 1980's showed a robot faking someone's voice on the phone as a warning that the Feds had developed the capability to do that. There weren't any terrorists hijacking airplanes armed with pocketknives. That part of the lie was aimed at me; to keep me from carrying a pocketknife. The other parts of the lie gave them excuses to do what they wanted to do; attack Afghanistan and impose a police state. President Bush took advantage of it to attack Iraq.

There isn't any war against terrorism; it's a war against freedom. The conspiracy committing the terrorism is the same as the conspiracy imposing the police state. The terrorism is just to provide an excuse for the police state. The people in the World Trade Center were Mafia. The people in Afghanistan that were attacked in retaliation were Mafia. The people attacking them are Feds. It was exactly the same kill two birds with one stone technique as the assassination of President Kennedy.

The Feds from Russia attacked the Mafia in Afghanistan during the 1980's. Doesn't anyone remember that the mudjaheddin were the good guys back then? The Feds from the United States attacked the Mafia in Afghanistan in 2001, imposed a police state, and started torturing prisoners. Can't anyone tell that they are the bad guys? If you can't figure out that they are the bad guys, can't you figure out that they are lying?

It doesn't make a bit of sense for terrorists to attack the World Trade Center but not the White House and Capitol building. Whoever planned the attacks had enemies in the World Trade Center but friends and co-conspirators in the White House and Capitol building. It is ridiculous to think that untrained kamikaze pilots could fly those planes straight, level, at exactly the right altitude and with pinpoint accuracy into those buildings. Take a hundred untrained people to a flight simulator and see how many of them could get it right on the first attempt. It is much more believable that those airplanes flew straight, level, and right on target because they were guided missiles.

It isn't anything new for the Feds to use airplanes as guided missiles. During World War II the Feds began developing a technology for guiding bomber aircraft to their targets with a radar beam. After the war they continued developing it, perfected it, and used it to cause aircraft collisions. They used radar to find out the precise altitude, heading, and speed of an aircraft and then used a radar beam to guide another aircraft to collide with it. The crash that was called The Day The Music Died wasn't an accident; it was murder. So were several other aircraft collisions during the late

1950's and early 1960's. A book written in 1961 by a former airlines pilot has a code message in the prologue to tell conspirators that the Mafia had developed countermeasures to keep their planes from being hit. So the Feds quit doing it.

The vast majority of airplane crashes are deliberately caused. It's Russian roulette to fly on a commercial airliner because somebody might want it to crash. If the airliner you are on crashes at flying speed you do not have any chance of living through the crash because they fly so fast. Several different things could be done to improve safety, but the Feds won't allow them. When it was decided to have Doppler radar at airports to warn of wind shear, the Feds delayed the building program. If an airport doesn't have Doppler radar, then when a plane tries to land during a storm they can zap it with a Star Wars laser to make it crash and say that it must have been wind sheer. Airliners could carry large parachutes to parachute the entire plane to the ground, but the Feds won't allow it. They cause airliner crashes for the purpose of killing the people on the plane. They don't want anything to interfere with that.

RESTATEMENT POSTSCRIPT

I'm not the only person who knows that Russia is going to destroy the United States. Half of the inhabitants of the United States are conspirators who have been aware of it for years. The lower level Fed conspirators think that it isn't true; the Mafia and Nazi conspirators know that it is true. Russia has had the strategic capability to win a nuclear war with the United States since the late 1980's, primarily because of Star Wars lasers. The politicians and the high ranking military know that and they are keeping it a secret.

Do you have sense enough to learn from the lessons of history? In 1938 British Prime Minister Neville Chamberlain returned from Munich and said that Britain and Germany had agreed "never to go to war with one another again." A year later they were at war.

Politicians are conspirators. They aren't really working for the best interest of the people of their country. They are fighting for their conspiracy to rule the world. You cannot trust them to protect you. You must protect yourself. One of the reasons that Russia can destroy the United States and kill all of its inhabitants is that we do not have bomb shelters. The government policy not to build bomb shelters came from politicians deliberately committing treason. It's too late for the United States to build bomb shelters, but it isn't too late for other countries. Having a bomb shelter and a realistic warning system might save your life at the beginning of World War III. For Christians, the abomination of desolation is your early warning system. But the correct method of saving your life when Russia destroys the United States isn't to build a bomb shelter; it is to immigrate to another country before the attack.

A movie made 30 years ago says that they'll kill everyone in my family after this is published. But it's my responsibility to warn you about the nuclear war because no one else is going to. And this is a God-given opportunity to expose conspiracies and hypnosis. As for what's going to happen to me; you've seen that movie too. But I'm not any crazier than any other hypnotized person. When the atomic bombs explode, that will prove that I was telling the truth and all of the experts who said that I was crazy were lying. I expect the attack to occur during a recess of Congress within 40 days after they kill me.